[THE SOURCEBOOKS SHAKESPEARE]

The Taming of the Shrew

TEXT EDITOR
ANTONIA FORSTER

ADVISORY EDITORS
DAVID BEVINGTON AND PETER HOLLAND

SERIES EDITORS
MARIE MACAISA AND DOMINIQUE RACCAH

William Shakspeare

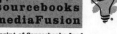
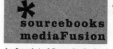

sourcebooks
mediaFusion

An Imprint of Sourcebooks Inc.®
Naperville, Illinois

Published by Sourcebooks MediaFusion, an imprint of Sourcebooks, Inc.
P.O. Box 4410, Naperville, Illinois 60567-4410
(630) 961-3900
Fax: (630) 961-2168
www.sourcebooks.com
www.sourcebooksshakespeare.com
For more information on The Sourcebooks Shakespeare, email us at shakespeare@sourcebooks.com.

Library of Congress Cataloging-in-Publication Data

Shakespeare, William, 1564-1616.
  The taming of the shrew / text editor, Antonia Forster ; advisory editors, David Bevington and Peter Holland.
    p. cm. — (The Sourcebooks Shakespeare)
  Includes bibliographical references.
  ISBN-13: 978-1-4022-0831-7 (alk. paper)
  ISBN-10: 1-4022-0831-6 (alk. paper)
  1. Man-woman relationships—Drama. 2. Married people—Drama. 3. Sex role—Drama. 4. Padua (Italy)—Drama. 5. Shakespeare, William, 1564-1616. Taming of the shrew. I. Forster, Antonia, 1951- II. Bevington, David M. III. Holland, Peter, 1951- IV. Title.
  PR2832.A2F67 2008
  822.3'3—dc22

                              2008003142

Printed and bound in the United States of America.
BVG 10 9 8 7 6 5 4 3 2 1

To students, teachers, and lovers of Shakespeare

Contents

About Sourcebooks MediaFusion

Launched with the 1998 *New York Times* bestseller *We Interrupt This Broadcast* and formally founded in 2000, Sourcebooks MediaFusion is the nation's leading publisher of mixed-media books. This revolutionary imprint is dedicated to creating original content—be it audio, video, CD-ROM, or Web—that is fully integrated with the books we create. The result, we hope, is a new, richer, eye-opening, thrilling experience with books for our readers. Our experiential books have become both bestsellers and classics in their subjects, including poetry (*Poetry Speaks*), children's books (*Poetry Speaks to Children*), history (*We Shall Overcome*), sports (*And The Crowd Goes Wild*), the plays of William Shakespeare, and more. See what's new from us at www.sourcebooks.com.

ABOUT THE TEXT

There are two versions of *Shrew*, a quarto of 1594 and a folio of 1623 (the First Folio). This text faithfully follows the folio, but reverts to the quarto for Sly's return (1.1.237SD–243). I have modernized along the principles espoused in Stanley Wells's *Modernizing Shakespeare's Spelling* (Oxford: Clarendon Press, 1979) and his *Re-Editing Shakespeare for the Modern Reader: Based on Lectures Given at the Folger Shakespeare Library, Washington, D.C.* (Oxford and New York: Clarendon Press; Oxford University Press, 1984). The folio's Exit has sometimes been silently emended to Exeunt; however, the folio's use of "and", often modernized to "an", has been retained.

Lineations for this play present some difficulties. Some editors have reset whole chunks of folio verse as prose, and, on rarer occasion, reset prose as verse, or neatened or conflated lines of unmetrical verse. Having consulted the First Folio (1623), Malone and Boswell the Younger's variorum edition (1821), Collier's edition (1878), as well as modern editions, including Brian Morris' Arden (1981), Oliver's Oxford text (1982), Frances E. Dolan's Bedford edition (1996), and Anne Thompson's New Cambridge edition (2003), I found wide variances and, often, no justification for overruling the First Folio. Listing the various preferences of these editions is not especially valuable in this edition, since none of these prose or verse preferences affects meaning. In the end, I decided that unless a strong majority of modern editors were in agreement, I would rely, as much as I could, on the First Folio, hoping, perhaps fruitlessly, that some of Shakespeare's original intention survived the various exigencies of the printhouse.

Editorial discussions of substantive readings are found in my commentaries; all editorial additions to the text are indicated in the notes. All Shakespeare quotations concerning other plays are derived from the aforementioned *The Riverside Shakespeare*, eds. G. Blakemore Evans and J.J.M. Tobin. 2nd ed. (Boston and New York: Houghton Mifflin Company, 1997) except where the Sourcebooks Shakespeare editions exist. References to eighteenth-century editions are culled from Malone and Boswell the Younger's *The Plays and Poems of William Shakespeare*, vol.V (London: F.C. and J. Rivington, etc.

1821). As for references to stage productions, I fully acknowledge my debt to Elizabeth Schafer's outstanding edition of *Shakespeare in Production: The Taming of the Shrew* (Cambridge: Cambridge, 2002).

Antonia Forster

On the CD

1. Introduction to the Sourcebooks Shakespeare *The Taming of the Shrew:* Sir Derek Jacobi

ACT 1, SCENE 1, LINES 48-103
2. Narration: Sir Derek Jacobi
3. Norman Tyrrell as Baptista, Sian Phillips as Katharina, Doria Noar as Bianca, and Ensemble
   Living Shakespeare • 1961
4. Sean Baker as Baptista, Frances Barber as Kate, Elizabeth Anne O'Brien as Bianca, and Ensemble
   The Complete Arkangel Shakespeare • 2003

ACT 2, SCENE 1, LINES 8-36
5. Narration: Sir Derek Jacobi
6. Norman Tyrrell as Baptista, Sian Phillips as Katharina, and Doria Noar as Bianca
   Living Shakespeare • 1961

ACT 2, SCENE 1, LINES 178-213
7. Narration: Sir Derek Jacobi
8. Peter O'Toole as Petruchio and Sian Phillips as Katharina
   Living Shakespeare • 1961
9. Roger Allam as Petruchio and Frances Barber as Kate
   The Complete Arkangel Shakespeare • 2003

ACT 2, SCENE 1, LINES 265-313
10. Narration: Sir Derek Jacobi
11. Roger Allam as Petruchio, Sean Baker as Baptista, Frances Barber as Kate, and Ensemble
    The Complete Arkangel Shakespeare • 2003
12. Marc Singer as Petruchio, William Paterson as Baptista, Fredi Olster as Katherina, and Ensemble
    Thirteen/WNET New York, Great Performances • 1976

ACT 5, SCENE 2, LINES 136-180
28. Narration: Sir Derek Jacobi
29. Sian Phillips as Katharina
    Living Shakespeare • 1961
30. Fredi Olster as Katherina
    Thirteen/WNET New York, Great Performances • 1976
31. Frances Barber as Kate
    The Complete Arkangel Shakespeare • 2003

32. Introduction to Speaking Shakespeare: Sir Derek Jacobi
33. Speaking Shakespeare: Andrew Wade with Myra Lucretia Taylor

34. Conclusion of the Sourcebooks Shakespeare *The Taming of the Shrew:* Sir Derek Jacobi

Featured Audio Productions

THE COMPLETE ARKANGEL SHAKESPEARE (2003)

Kate	Frances Barber
Petruchio	Roger Allam
Lucentio	Alan Cox
Tranio	Clarence Smith
Hortensio	Charles Simpson
Baptista	Sean Baker
Gremio	John Hollis
Bianca	Elizabeth Anne O'Brien
Grumio	Michael Higgs
Vincentio	Keith Drinkel
Pedant	Michael Deacon
Widow	Jenny Howe
Biondello	Richard Pearce
Tailor	Robert Morgan
Curtis	Max Digby

Directed by Clive Brill

THIRTEEN/WNET NEW YORK, GREAT PERFORMANCES: THEATER IN AMERICA (1976)

Katherina	Fredi Olster
Petruchio	Marc Singer
Baptista	William Paterson
Bianca	Sandra Shotwell
Lucentio	Stephen St. Paul
Gremio	Raye Birk
A Pedant	Earl Boen
Grumio	Ronald Boussom
Sugarsop	Barbara Dirickson
Haberdasher	Bobby F. Ellerbee
Mariamo	Harry Hamlin
Tranio	Rick Hamilton
Camellio	Charles Hyman
Biondello	Daniel Kern
Emilio	Michael Keys Hall
A Widow	Deborah May
Nathaniel	Al White
Vincentio	Laird Williamson
Hortensio	James R. Winkler
Tailor	Daniel Zippi

Clowns: Frank Abe, Tomas Arana, Lynn Butler, Melodie Butler, Peter Davies, Nancy Erskine, Suzanne Fry, Marc Hayashi, Joy Juvelis, Rodney Kageyama, David Kudler, Eric Nelson, John Salat, Suzie Smith, Jean Trounstine, Althea Watson, Susan Westerman, Kathy Wong
Directed by Kirk Browning, based on the original stage production directed by William Ball

LIVING SHAKESPEARE (1961)

Lucentio	Robin Phillips
Tranio	Harry Locke
Baptista	Norman Tyrrell
Gremio	Kenneth Griffith
Katharina	Sian Phillips
Hortensio	Richard Gale

Bianca	Doria Noar
Petruchio	Peter O'Toole
Grumio	Henry Woolf
Biondello	John Davidson
Curtis	Peter Birrel
Haberdasher	Peter Birrel
Vincentio	Peter Birrel
Directed by John Hale	

CANADIAN BROADCASTING SYSTEM (1961)
The Taming of the Shrew originally produced as part of the CBC radio adaptations series
No credits available

Note from the Series Editors

For many of us, our first and only encounter with Shakespeare was in school. We may recall that experience as a struggle, working through dense texts filled with unfamiliar words. However, those of us who were fortunate enough to have seen a play performed have altogether different memories. It may be of an interesting scene or an unusual character, but it is most likely a speech. Often, just hearing part of one instantly transports us to that time and place. "Friends, Romans, countrymen, lend me your ears," "But, soft! What light through yonder window breaks?," "To sleep, perchance to dream," "Tomorrow, and tomorrow, and tomorrow."

The Sourcebooks Shakespeare series is our attempt to use the power of performance to help you experience the play. In it, you will see photographs from various productions, on film and on stage, historical and contemporary, known worldwide or in your community. You may even recognize some actors you don't think of as Shakespearean performers. You will see set drawings, costume designs, and scene edits, all reproduced from original notes. Finally, on the enclosed audio CD, you will hear scenes from the play as performed by some of the most accomplished Shakespeareans of our times. Often, we include multiple interpretations of the same scene, showing you the remarkable richness of the text. Hear Peter O'Toole's Petruchio and Sian Phillips's Katharina from the 1961 Living Shakespeare series first encounter each other in the famous wooing scene (2.1.178-313). Compare their scene with that of Marc Singer and Fredi Olster as Petruchio and Katherina from the American Conservatory Theatre's 1976 rowdy commedia dell'arte production. The actors create different worlds, different characters, different meanings.

As you read the text of the play, you can consult explanatory notes for definitions of unfamiliar words and phrases or words whose meanings have changed. These notes appear on the left pages, next to the text of the play. The audio, photographs, and other production artifacts augment the notes and they too are indexed to the appropriate lines. You can use the pictures to see how others have staged a particular scene and get ideas on costumes, scenery, blocking, etc. As for the audio, each track represents a particular interpretation of a scene. Sometimes, a passage that's difficult to comprehend opens up when you hear it out loud. Furthermore, when you hear more than one version, you gain a keener understanding of the characters. Is Petruchio a misogynist? Has Katherina truly been tamed? Are they, after all, in love? The actors made their choices and so can you. You may even come up with your own interpretation.

The text of the play, the definitions, the production notes, the audio—all of these work together, and they are included for your enjoyment. Because the audio consists of performance excerpts, it is meant to entertain. When you see a passage with an associated clip, you can read along as you hear the actors perform the scenes for you. Or, you can sit back, close your eyes, and listen, and then go back and reread the text with a new perspective. Finally, since the text is actually a script, you may find yourself reciting the lines out loud and doing your own performance!

You will undoubtedly notice that some of the audio does not exactly match the text. Also, there are photographs and facsimiles of scenes that aren't in your edition. There are many reasons for this, but foremost among them is the fact that Shakespeare scholarship continues to move forward and the prescribed ways of dealing with and interpreting text is always changing. Thus a play that was edited and published in the 1900s will be different from one published in 2008. Finally, artists have their own interpretation of the play and they too cut and change lines and scenes according to their vision.

The ways in which *The Taming of the Shrew* has been presented have varied considerably through the years. We've included essays in the book to give you glimpses into the range of the productions, showing you how other artists have approached the play and providing examples of just what changes were made and how. Christy Desmet writes of William Ball's prize-winning production at the American Conservatory Theatre in 1976. She describes how Ball's fundamental approach made the play's language shine. Performers at the ACT took classes not only in dance, singing, and fencing, but also in scansion (the art of reading verse) and phonetics, improving their technical focus on the spoken word and enhancing the actors' delivery, their comic repartee, and the audience's comprehension of Shakespearean verse. Antonia Forster, our text editor, provides an overview of how the play has been performed through the years, discussing the complications posed by not only the plot but also the existence of an alternate version, *The Taming of A Shrew*. Douglas Lanier cites quite a few adaptations of the play in popular culture, showing how the play's central plot has played into different genres and cultures (e.g., Westerns and Hispanic *Shrews*) as well as into sexual politics, where various productions have scrambled the genders, rendering the man the shrew and the woman the tamer. Finally, for the actor in you, (and for those who want to peek behind the curtain), we have an essay that you may find especially intriguing. Andrew Wade, voice coach of the Royal Shakespeare Company for sixteen years, shares his point of view on how to understand the text and speak it. You can also listen in on him working with an actor on a speech of the play; perhaps you too can learn the art of speaking Shakespeare.

One last note: we are frequently asked why we didn't include the whole play, either in audio or video. While we enjoy the plays and are avid theatergoers, we are trying to do something more with the audio (and the production notes and the essays) than just presenting them to you. In fact, our goal is to provide you tools that will enable you to explore the play on your own, from many different directions. Our hope is that the different pieces of audio, the voices of the actors, and the old production photos and notes will all engage you and illuminate the play on many levels, so that you can construct your own understanding and create your own "production," a fresh interpretation unique to you.

Though the productions we referenced and the audio clips we have included are but a miniscule sample of the play's history, we hope they encourage you to further delve into the works of Shakespeare. New editions of the play come out yearly; movie adaptations are regularly being produced; there are hundreds of theater groups in the U.S. alone; and performances could be going on right in your backyard. We echo the words of noted writer and poet Robert Graves, who said, "The remarkable thing about Shakespeare is that

he is really very good—in spite of all the people who say he is very good."
We welcome you now to The Sourcebooks Shakespeare edition of *The Taming of the Shrew.*

Dominique Raccah and Marie Macaisa
Series Editors

Introduction to the Sourcebooks Shakespeare *The Taming of the Shrew*
Sir Derek Jacobi

track 1

In Production
The Taming of the Shrew THROUGH THE YEARS

Antonia Forster

Reviewing the Royal Shakespeare Company's 2003 production of *The Taming of the Shrew* in *Shakespeare Bulletin*, Thomas Larque comments that director Gregory Doran "knows very well that *The Taming of the Shrew* is one of the most difficult plays to stage for a modern audience" (1). Indeed, throughout its performance history, productions have struggled to address the bawdiness and excesses of the play by adapting it, reinterpreting its characterizations, or pairing its performance with its contemporary feminist counterpart. The latter was Doran's approach: Larque stated that Doran "tries to answer condemnations of the play as woman-hating and repulsive by pairing it with Fletcher's proto-feminist sequel *The Tamer Tamed*" (*The Woman's Prize, or The Tamer Tamed*, c. 1611), in which Petruchio is tamed. Linking the two plays goes further back than modern sensibilities' problems with *Shrew*, however. The first definite recorded performance of *The Taming of the Shrew* (in 1633, four decades after it was written), at court for King Charles I and Queen Henrietta Maria, was in conjunction with *The Tamer Tamed*. The records of Sir Henry Herbert, Master of the Revels, show that while *Shrew* was "likt", *The Tamer Tamed* was "Very well likt". Even John Lacy's adaptation of the play, *Sauny the Scot* (1667), concludes with Petruchio linking the two as well:

> I've *Tam'd the Shrew*, but will not be asham'd,
> If next you see the very *Tamer Tam'd*.

Theatre Manager Philip Henslowe's diary records a performance of *The Tamynge of a Shrew* at Newington Butts on June 13, 1594, but scholars contest whether or not the play, known in scholarly circles as *A Shrew*, is the same play (referred to as *The Shrew*) published in the First Folio of Shakespeare's plays in 1623. Confusion on this point has complicated the early history of Shakespeare's play, and to this day, multiple theories of origin surround its study, three of which are particularly prominent: 1) that *A Shrew* represents and early version of Shakespeare's later play, 2) that *A Shrew* and *The Shrew* are both based on an earlier play that has since been lost, or 3) that Shakespeare based *The Shrew* on the earlier play *A Shrew*. Stemming from the first theory described above, some have argued what is known as the "bad quarto" theory, which suggests that *A Shrew* is a faulty copy of Shakespeare's original text published from memory (2). These are not the only theories, and the murky tangle among them makes dating, sources, and stage history problematic.

As Tori Haring-Smith points out in *From Farce to Metadrama*, "The next two hundred and fifty years of the stage history of *The Taming of the Shrew* have remarkably little to do with Shakespeare" (3). Although several adaptations of the play were popular during that time—including John Lacy's *The Sauny Scot* (1667) and two farces both called *The Cobbler of Preston* and based on the Christopher Sly episodes—Shakespeare's *Shrew* was not seen in a recognizable form until David Garrick produced a pared-down version in 1754, *Catharine and Petruchio*.

Whereas *Sauny the Scot* maintained many aspects of *Shrew* (but with altered setting and most of the names changed), Garrick omitted many characters and removed the bawdiness but did no re-naming. His play focused on the main plot, dispensing with the subplot of Bianca and her suitors. Garrick also cast the taming and the relationship between Catharine and Petruchio in a different light by ending the play with Catharine delivering not a 44-line speech, but four short ones (the longest of 9 lines and the shortest of 2), only two of them from the original play. She is also interrupted by Petruchio, Bianca, and Baptista, with Baptista offering a second dowry and Petruchio refusing it, stating that his "Fortune is sufficient" and Catharine is his wealth. Furthermore, Petruchio paints a future of equality now that she has become so "prudent, kind, and dutiful a Wife":

> *Petruchio* here shall doff the lordly Husband;
> An honest Mask, which I throw off with Pleasure.
> Far hence all Rudeness, Wilfulness, and Noise,
> And be our future Lives one gentle Stream
> Of mutual Love, Compliance and Regard.

The final lines are his, as, holding Catharine by the hand, he delivers ten lines of her speech from the original play (5.2.155-164).

For nearly a century, Garrick's version was the only version of the play on the stage in Britain or the United States. In 1808 Thomas Davies, Garrick's biographer, recorded Garrick's view that the original play "was not altogether written in Shakespeare's best manner, though it contained many scenes well worth preserving" and maintained that the "loppings from this luxuriant tree were not only judicious, but necessary to preserve the pristine trunk." Much later, George C. D. Odell, surveying *Shakespeare from Betterton to Irving* (1920), describes Garrick's "excellent farce" as "compact and actable to a degree" and deserving of its popularity as an afterpiece which it maintained until it was "driven from the stage" in 1886 (1887, according to Tori Haring-Smith) with the revival of the full play in the United States by Augustin Daly and his company.

When further rewriting took place, it was Garrick's version that was adapted. John Philip Kemble, for example, produced a version popular on the stage and entitled, in its 1810 publication, *Shakspeare's Katharine and Petruchio, a Comedy; taken by David Garrick from The Taming of a Shrew: revised by J. P. Kemble* (the 1786 publication does not mention Kemble's name but does note *Marked with the Variations in the Manager's Book, at the Theatre-Royal in Covent Garden*). In 1854 F. C. Wemyss prefaced his New York edition of *Katharine and Petruchio* by saying that it has "retained Possession of the Stage as an especial favourite for a hundred years" while *Shrew* "has been consigned to the shelves of the library." In 1878 William Winter, editing Edwin Booth's alteration of Garrick's play, observes that Shakespeare's original play "is never acted" and that "adapting it to the modern stage" has led to the rejection of a large part of it, but by then there had been several productions of the full play in England and, a decade later the situation had changed in the United States too. The first performance of the complete play (with only twenty-five lines cut, as the prompt book in the Folger Library shows) was at the Haymarket Theatre in London in 1844 with J. R. Planché using the scholarship of Edmond Malone and John Payne Collier to provide information on Elizabethan staging which he tried to follow as much as possible. Thus, in the nineteenth century, the restoration of Shakespeare's original play alternated with *Katharine and Petruchio*, and the influence of Garrick continued into the twentieth century.

Miriam Gilbert observes in 2005 that in more than 40 years of productions of the play by the Royal Shakespeare Company, she sees "a series of performance strategies aimed at making the play not merely enjoyable but intellectually and emotionally satisfying"; this description could be extended to cover much of the twentieth century's engagement with performance of the play. Beginning in the nineteenth century and increasing massively since the 1960s, the uneasiness felt by earlier periods concerning the bawdiness and excesses of the plots was replaced by uneasiness about the play's attitude to women. This uneasiness was perhaps most famously expressed in Michael

Billington's much-quoted question in the *Guardian* in 1978 (responding to Bogdanov's production mentioned below) about "whether there is any reason to revive a play that seems totally offensive to our age and our society," which he answered by saying that the play "should be put back firmly and squarely on the shelf." If the play was often seen, as in his review, as "barbaric and disgusting," that is also part of the reason for its popularity. As Ann Thompson said in her Cambridge edition (2003), "from the very beginning it has been disturbing as well as enjoyable." Likewise, John Elsom said in 1989, presenting two extremes, that "at different times and places, it has been presented either as good marriage guidance or as a skilful send-up of male chauvinist dreams"; few would now try the former, even if they believe it to have been Shakespeare's view, and many modern productions have naturally attempted the latter, while others have tried to negotiate a position which is neither.

Through the twentieth century and beyond, the play has been popular on film and on the stage. In 1929 Sam Taylor directed and co-wrote a film version starring Mary Pickford and her then husband, Douglas Fairbanks. Pickford later wrote that making the film was a frustrating and unhappy experience that finished her and that Fairbanks turned into a real-life Petruchio.

The film, the first Shakespeare "talkie," was also released in a silent version and is full of large gestures and extended action; in it the focus is as much on Kate as on Petruchio and, despite her pouting and often almost parodically "little woman" demeanour, this Kate has many strengths and is certainly not tamed. Her wink at her sister following her exaggerated (but greatly cut) final speech of submission has been much discussed and imitated and has influenced many subsequent approaches to the meaning of this speech and consequently to the play as a whole.

The most widely seen production of the play, still generally available forty years later, is Franco Zeffirelli's 1966 film starring Elizabeth Taylor and Richard Burton. As with the Pickford/Fairbanks version, some public reaction was clearly conditioned by the famous real-life relationship between the two leading actors which had received vast media coverage. Zeffirelli considerably softens the impact of the "taming" with a great deal of cutting, violence that is farcical, and a Petruchio whose tenderness and uncertainty are intermittently visible under his bluster. Petruchio's obvious nervousness during the playing-out of the bet near the end makes it clear that he is by no means sure what Kate will do, and his stifled surprise is as clear as his delight when she performs as a perfect, dutiful wife. This is not unusual; Elizabeth

Mary Pickford as Katherina in the 1929 film directed by Sam Taylor
Photo Courtesy of Douglas Lanier

Schafer's *Shakespeare in Production* notes give several examples of "very anxious" Petruchios at the point when Kate re-enters. In fact Zeffirelli later wrote that both he and Burton were surprised by Taylor's straight and unironic performance of her final speech.

In the theatre, Michael Bogdanov's 1978 Royal Shakespeare Company production threw the audience's expectations in their faces when he began

Elizabeth Taylor as Kate and Richard Burton as Petruchio
The 1967 Film directed by Franco Zeffirelli
© 1967 Columbia Pictures Corporation, Courtesy of Douglas Lanier

with a surprisingly traditional decorative set soon destroyed by a drunk who had pushed aside an usher and jumped onto the stage. As Michael Billington reported, "gullible patrons" began rushing off to call the police, but the drunk turned out to be Sly (Jonathan Price, also playing Petruchio) and the usher, Paola Dionisotti, came back as Kate. The destruction of the old-fashioned set in this violent modern-dress production, as various commentators pointed out, paralleled the destruction or mockery of the historical reconstructions and costumes more usually seen. Bogdanov's view is that Shakespeare "was a feminist" and that in the play "his sympathy is with the women, and his purpose, to expose the cruelty of a society that allows these things to happen."

Two years after Bogdanov's production came Jonathan Miller's film in the BBC /Time-Life Shakespeare series with Sarah Badel and John Cleese in the two leading parts. John Cleese's fame as a comedy actor in *Monty Python's Flying Circus* and *Fawlty Towers* gave Petruchio a comic resonance before he even opened his mouth and thus, in a sense, drew part of the sting of Petruchio's treatment of Kate. However, Jonathan Miller says in the BBC's text:

> I was interested in certain aspects of Elizabethan Puritanism—
> the Puritan squirearchy and the idea of the moral seriousness of
> Petruchio rather than his cavalierish twinkle, which is the usual
> way it is done. There's a certain sort of moral gravity, which I
> think is actually there in Cleese: underneath the fun and humour
> of the man there is an intensity.

Miller, who had earlier directed a stage production at Chichester with Joan Plowright and Anthony Hopkins and in 1987 did another with Fiona Shaw and Brian Cox, was strongly opposed to seeing the play as being about women's liberation or repression, and in several places, including his *Subsequent Performances* (1986), expressed scorn for directors like Joseph Papp who turned the play into "a test case for feminism" and made Kate's final speech ironic. He saw the play as part of its own time, not ours, and rejected attempts to "frog-march Shakespeare into the twentieth century." Graham Holderness remarked in 1989 on the way John Cleese's delivery of Petruchio's Act 2 and Act 4 soliloquies (2.1.164-177, 4.1.158-181) makes the speeches into "meditative self-communings, introverted self-interrogations absorbedly unaware of listeners or spectators" and thus "naturalistic representations of a psychological process of self-examination and moral inquiry."

Sarah Badel, whose delivery of Kate's final speech is calm and loving, comments in the BBC text that she sees Kate as a woman with "enormous capacity for love" and the speech as a "love speech" to Petruchio as she has now realized "the extreme vulnerability of men."

Gale Edwards' 1995 production for the Royal Shakespeare Company (with Josie Lawrence and Michael Siberry) attracted considerable attention even before it opened because it was the first *Shrew* directed by a woman on the main stage there. Edwards later expressed herself in strong terms on the impossibility of meeting critical expectations for a woman directing the play and the certainty of being criticized for being both too feminist and not feminist enough. There were some vicious reviews, directed particularly at the cuts and alterations (e.g., at the end of the play-within-the-play, Petruchio had lost Kate and was distraught), some of which involved using the frame-closing material from *A Shrew*, hardly a reprehensibly new idea.

The 2003 RSC production that paired the play with *The Tamer Tamed*, both starring Alexandra Gilbreath and Jasper Britton, also aroused a great deal of interest because of the rethinking engendered by the linking of the two plays. It was not only the pairing, however, that caused a re-estimation of *Shrew*. Georgina Brown, writing in *The Mail on Sunday* about *Shrew* alone, reported having earlier vowed never again to endure a production of this "repellent and misogynist" play, but was won over completely by Doran's "thoughtful portrait of a marriage" and its moving presentation of

Alexandra Gilbreath as Maria and Jasper Britton as Petruchio in the 2003 Royal Shakespeare Company production of *The Tamer Tamed* written by John Fletcher
Photo: Donald Cooper

two people who have been transformed by their relationship. John Peter in the *Sunday Times* had never "seen this relationship played with more intelligence and sheer excitement," and there was a great deal of favorable comment. Remarking on the ways in which the production could both "question and affirm the couple's current—and future—rapport", Miriam Gilbert reports Alexandra Gilbreath's observation that the paired productions gave the actors "the luxury of being able to play *Shrew* on its own terms, without feeling that they had to invent a happy ending to make it palatable."

During the past century, and particularly the past thirty years, one of the major problems in the performance of *The Taming of the Shrew* has been the end of the play. Is the frame closed, using or adapting the end of *A Shrew*? Many productions have done so, and this has helped to achieve a distance from or comment on the play itself, clarifying some of the difficult issues. It may, as in Gale Edwards' production, transform the play-within-the-play into a dream. What do we make of Katherina's final speech? Is she being sarcastic? Does she mean what she says? If so, what exactly is she saying? The answers affect the impact of the play. The range of options in performance is enormous, from sincere self-abasement to the irony suggested by the winking first made popular by Mary Pickford or the extreme point conveyed by a 1986 Turkish production in which Katherina died, having cut her wrist and bled to death. Whether seen as a "nostalgic fantasy" in which women are shown their proper place or a difficult and almost unplayable outrage against women or something in between, *The Taming of the Shrew* remains popular with audiences, challenging to directors, and interesting to scholars.

Notes:

(1) See Thomas Larque, "*Taming of the Shrew*, Royal Shakespeare Company, (Performed 2003)", in *Shakespeare Bulletin* 21.4 (Winter 2003): 76–79.

(2) See Stephen Roy Miller's introduction to the 1998 Cambridge edition of the play, which provides detailed information about the play's nature and history, offering documentation and possibilities to support his theory that *A Shrew* represents Shakespeare's early draft of *The Shrew*.

(3) Tori Haring-Smith. *From Farce to Metadrama: A Stage History of the Taming of the Shrew*. (Westport, CT: Greenwood Press, 1985).

Grateful acknowledgments are due to the Folger Shakespeare Library and its staff, without whom the research for this essay would have been a far poorer thing, and to three books in particular: Tori Haring-Smith, *From Farce to Metadrama: a Stage History of The Taming of the Shrew, 1594-1983* (Westport, CT and London: Greenwood, 1985); Graham Holderness, *Shakespeare in Performance: The Taming of the Shrew* (Manchester and New York: Manchester UP, 1989); and Elizabeth Schafer's edition of *Shrew* in the *Shakespeare in Production* series (Cambridge UP, 2002). In addition, two essays in *A Companion to Shakespeare and Performance* ed. Barbara Hodgdon and W. B. Worthen (Oxford: Blackwell, 2005) have been very helpful: "Performance as Deflection" by Miriam Gilbert and "Maverick Shakespeare" by Carol Chillington Rutter. I have also benefited from information in John Elsom ed. *Is Shakespeare Still our Contemporary?* (London and New York; Routledge, 1989), Elizabeth Schafer, *Ms-Directing Shakespeare: Women Direct Shakespeare* (London: The Women's Press, 1998), and Marcela Kostihovà, "Katherina 'humanized': Abusing the Shrew on the Prague stage." *World-wide Shakespeares: Local appropriations in films and performance.* Ed. Sonia Massai. (London and New York: Routledge, 2005).

As Performed: The Taming of the Shrew

By The American Conservatory Theatre (ACT) in San Francisco, CA, in 1976 and filmed for the PBS Great Performances series

Christy Desmet

In an exchange conducted online (http://www.shaksper.net/), a number of scholars responded to a request for a good film version of *The Taming of the Shrew*. Though not all of them remembered the complete details, they all recalled a televised version that had been intelligent and very funny. The *Shrew* they remembered was produced by the American Conservatory Theatre (ACT) under the direction of William Ball and broadcast in 1976 by Public Broadcasting System (PBS) as part of its Great Performances program. Aside from providing an accessible introduction to Shakespeare's *The Taming of the Shrew*, this particular production is noteworthy for several reasons, beginning with the fortuitous match between play and theater company.

Founder William Ball's American Conservatory Theatre represents a uniquely American foray into classical theatrical training and performance. Tired of the financial pressures in the Broadway theater world, William Ball acquired funds from the Rockefeller Foundation to construct a regional company dedicated to high artistic standards rather than commercial success. He founded the American Conservatory Theatre in 1965 and moved the company from Pittsburgh to San Francisco in 1967. True to Ball's artistic vision, ACT became a repertory company (one that offers a number of plays in continuous rotation during a given season) and a conservatory inspired by the great national theater conservatories of Europe. According to Ball's vision, the actors involved in ACT's productions worked for extended periods of times—as much as three or four years at a stretch—studying continuously, perfecting the company's repertory works and teaching younger professionals in the conservatory where Ball himself was an active teacher. Because of the company's rigorous training, the 1976 film version of *Shrew* demonstrates the ACT's signature style, for before the production was filmed, it was part of the company's repertoire during the 1973-74, 1974-75, and 1975-76 seasons.

Several qualities of the ACT *Shrew* distinguish it among acted and filmed versions of the play. First, whereas drama destined for television was usually filmed in the studio, this performance took place on a nearly bare stage before a live audience, giving viewers a sense of the conditions and constraints under which the company operated and demonstrating the power of the audience response during live comedy. Second, Ball's fundamental approach to technical action gave room for the play's language to shine. Because ACT repertory performers and students at the conservatory took classes in not only dance, singing, and fencing, but also in scansion (the art of reading verse) and phonetics, their technical focus on the spoken word enhanced the actors' delivery of and the audience's comprehension of the production's Shakespearean verse and comic repartee. Finally, and perhaps most importantly, by virtue of the ACT's trademark acting style and the production's use of *commedia del arte* conventions, the William Ball *Shrew* negotiates a potentially treacherous path through the play's gender politics, which have posed problems for contemporary viewers and theatergoers in Shakespeare's own day.

CRITICAL ATTITUDES TOWARD SHAKESPEARE'S SHREW TAMING

Performers and literary critics tend to approach Shakespeare's *The Taming of the Shrew* from one of three largely incompatible perspectives. According to the first line of argument, *Shrew* is a farce whose humor depends on slapstick violence. Because the characters and caricatures and neither represents a "real" person, we can laugh at Petruchio's taming of Kate without worrying about the implications of wife-beating, starvation, and social deprivation that Petruchio employs to make his "haggard" come at his call (4.1.163-164). The second approach concedes that Kate is tamed but maintains that this educational process is meant for her own good and ensures the marital happiness of husband and wife. To some extent, this approach is pre-feminist, acknowledging the patriarchal structure of the post-Reformation English family and the idea that a husband, as the head of that family, is in Katherina's words "lord", "king", and "governor" of the family (5.2.138). A softer variant of this argument suggests that Shakespeare's *The Taming of the Shrew* does not so much reflect Renaissance misogyny as it does an emerging Protestant doctrine of companionate marriage in which man and wife have complementary duties, working together for the material and spiritual health of the family. A third approach hails Kate as a heroine and argues that she successfully manipulates male expectations for female obedience to achieve independence and even mastery over Petruchio without relinquishing the pleasures of love, sex, and social status. Replacing the institution of marriage with an emphasis on love, William Ball's production matches physical comedy with a strong sense of sexual chemistry between Petruchio and Kate to combine the first line of argument's emphasis on physical farce with the third's celebration of Kate as the play's heroine. The production hardly examines marriage as an institution, and shifting the context from marriage to love allows viewers to balance their enjoyment of the play's comic action with their affection for and appreciation of its principal lovers.

CHARACTER, VIOLENCE, AND METADRAMA IN WILLIAM BALL'S *Shrew*

William Ball's *Taming of the Shrew* draws on character types, costumes, and comic routines from the Italian *commedia dell'arte* tradition that flourished in Italy during Shakespeare's lifetime, mixed perhaps with some antics from 1930s screwball film comedies and cartoon sound effects. With characters and action thus stylized, the audience is given plenty of opportunity to laugh without considering the play's social subtext too seriously. Like the *commedia* tradition, *Shrew* pits young people against old, to the detriment of the latter. Lucentio and Biondello refer casually to Bianca's father as an "old pantaloon" whom they "beguile" without qualms in pursuit of romance (3.1.35). Bianca's unsuitable lover Gremio—whose breath stuns men and women alike in the Ball production and who suffers repeatedly the indignity of having his cane kicked out from underneath him—is a classic pantaloon: a ridiculous, old man who inappropriately seeks to possess the romantic heroine through his wealth and whose humiliation is roundly cheered by the audience. The pedant who impersonates Lucentio's father is yet another pantaloon. By choosing stylized characters over real individuals, the production directs our affection and attention to the young lovers and legitimizes their triumph over patriarchal law.

The American Conservatory Theatre's use of ensemble acting also works to draw the audience's sympathy to Shakespeare's young lovers. As the term "ensemble acting" suggests, at least to Ball's American Conservatory Theater, group effects were more important than individuals; there were to be no stars, and the theatrical style was consistent throughout the troupe. While some film productions focus purely on Kate and Petruchio, the ACT fully represented the tripled love plots of Shakespeare's *Shrew* to highlight not simply the triumph of youth over age, but also Kate and Petruchio's superior vitality as characters and lovers. In the romantic competitions that take center stage in the Ball production, Kate and Petruchio are clearly the winners, in more than a financial sense. Bianca and Lucentio are stereotypes drawn equally from the Italian *commedia* and sonnet traditions. We laugh at their gulling of the Baptista in the service of true love, but Lucentio and Bianca's lack of responsibility and intellectual deficits only serve to highlight the wit and energy of Kate and Petruchio, who paradoxically turn out to the better citizens in Shakespearean Padua. Hortensio's effete, languid character (reinforced by a teeth-jarring giggle) and his widow's last-minute adoption of the shrew role work as well to draw our sympathies to Kate and Petruchio as the play's principal and most endearing lovers.

Finally, Ball's production uses both the audience, filmed as they watch the play, and an additional on-stage audience to enhance the play's comic ethos. The performance of *Shrew* before a live audience makes this film energetic and interactive. The presence of spectators is supplemented by an onstage audience of masked *commedia dell'arte* musicians who mediate the larger audience's response. Like everyone else in the play, the onstage spectators are besotted with Bianca; they tease Baptista and generally add an air of carnival into the theatrical proceedings. For instance, they interject cheers at the ritualistic mention of "Padua" in Shakespeare's text and provide sound effects for the repeated stage gag in which any mention of Antonio (Petruchio's deceased

The Ensemble in the 1976 American Conservatory Theatre production directed by William Ball and filmed for PBS Great Performances
Photo courtesy of The American Conservatory Theatre

father) results in a reverential removal of hats, punctuated by musical gong sounds and finally, a discordant horn blast delivered by a rogue musician who, when singled out by the other performers, simply shrugs his shoulders.

So while William Ball's *Shrew*, like most filmed versions, eliminates the Christopher Sly frame that emotionally distances spectators from the taming plot and its characters, interaction between performers and an onstage audience emphasizes the meta-dramatic aspects of *Shrew*, which remind us periodically that we are witnessing a performance rather than reality. Such meta-dramatic moments, at least in the case of this *Shrew*, not only assure the audience that no real harm is being done but also suggest that the principal players, Kate and Petruchio, may themselves be accomplished actors hiding real emotions under absurd behavior. Neither Kate's shrewishness nor Petruchio's misogyny is "real", the production suggests, paving the way for a successful rapprochement between the lovers and setting the stage for their triumph over everyone else in the play.

KATE AND PETRUCHIO: "A COUPLE OF QUIET ONES"

The ACT's approach to its rambunctious lovers echoes Baptista's common-sense assertion that he seeks "quiet" in the match between Petruchio and Katharina (2.1.319), and ironic observation ("Let them go, a couple of quiet ones", 3.2.230) after their abrupt departure before the wedding feast. By the end of the play, Kate and Petruchio have learned to exploit the pleasures of dramatic performance while enjoying wealth and social stability; by all indications, they also achieve domestic harmony without relinquishing passion and sexual satisfaction.

Most crucial to an interpretation that valorizes Kate and Petruchio is the handling of the wife-taming that drives the play's action. The production softens the violence inherent to farce by stylizing *Shrew*'s dramatic action, both in the encounters between Kate and Petruchio and more generally throughout the performance. ACT's approach to dramatic character begins with "physical activity and works inward toward inner emotions" (Steele 1975, quoted in Wilk, 139). To some extent, physical engagement is ubiquitous in the production, so much so that the violence comes to look more like play than war. The "knock me here and knock me there" fisticuffs between Petruchio and Grumio (1.2.1–19), although potentially suggesting class-based violence between master and servant, ends with Hortensio reconciling the two men and offering the momentarily infantilized Grumio a sympathetic hug, which the servant then rewards with a resounding kiss on Hortensio's cheek.

Because of the ensemble's training in dance and movement, combat often approximated ballet. Kate and Petruchio's first encounter, generally

referred to as the "wooing scene" (2.1.178-269), is choreographed as an elaborate performance, part verbal contest and part wrestling match. The two
face off against one another from the beginning but meet frequently in the
middle with Petruchio's face framing Kate's as if for a prom photograph.
The appearance, costuming, stance, and gestures of Fredi Olster (Katherina) and Marc Singer (Petruchio) complement one another closely and
sometimes even mirror one another so accurately that we readily believe
they belong together. Throughout the scene, the two engage in adolescent
hi-jinks: she gives him a blow to the crotch and bites his hand, while he
reciprocates by stomping on her foot ("Why does the world report that Kate
doth limp?" 2.1.242). By the end of the scene, Petruchio is slinging Kate
back and forth in time to Shakespeare's verse, while she mugs to the camera in disbelief. Together, the two actors combine athletic agility (Marc
Singer actually has a black belt in Kung Fu) with a sexual display that is
at once excessive and endearing.

A traditional ploy for softening the violence of *The Taming of the Shrew*
is to signal love-at-first-sight between Kate and Petruchio. Ball chooses to
have Kate give a long, approving look at Petruchio's backside, which generally is clad in form-fitting tights that emphasize the muscularity of his thighs;
this dramatic pause culminates in a broad smile to the audience that Fredi
Olster's Kate immediately suppresses as she resumes her characteristically

Fredi Olster as Kate and Marc Singer as Petruchio and Ensemble in the 1976 American Conservatory
Theatre production directed by William Ball and filmed for PBS Great Performances
Photo courtesy of The American Conservatory Theatre

abrasive haughtiness with a flip of the wrist. Kate clearly likes what she sees. Marc Singer's Petruchio is made less threatening by a boyish haircut and silly grin combined with a comic, yet pleasingly hyper-masculine body. In the wooing scene, Singer not only wears his trademark form-fitting tights and sports the bare chest that allows film buffs to recognize him as the Beastmaster, he also displays an ample codpiece. Bianca's ancient wooer Gremio is reduced to quivers as he performs a rhetorical catalogue of Petruchio's body, punching his trim stomach and pinching his muscular arms before gazing in wonder at that codpiece. Olster's Kate, with her broad, beautiful facial features and a voluptuous décolletage, is at the same time athletic. She is Petruchio's perfect counterpart, both in physical type and verbal facility. We can agree readily with Baptista when he says, "'Tis a match!" (2.1.308).

By far the most difficult event for many contemporary spectators is Kate's long speech in praise of wifely obedience in Act 5 (5.2.136-179). Here, the appeals to conventions of farce or even to Renaissance attitudes about marriage will not suffice. When Kate offers to place her hand beneath Petruchio's foot in a sign of abject submission, the film's audience, like the guests at Lucentio's feast, can only gape. But Katherine's performance of those words is what matters. Her strong, mellifluous voice, broad hand gestures, and dramatic collapse at Petruchio's feet make Olster's Kate a Renaissance precursor to twentieth-century film actress Katherine Hepburn, at once

Ronald Boussom as Grumio and Marc Singer as Petruchio in the 1976 American Conservatory Theatre production directed by William Ball and filmed for PBS Great Performances
Photo courtesy of The American Conservatory Theatre

strong and seductive. The final effect is that Kate and Petruchio, whether they stand cheek-to-cheek as in their first encounter or rise from the floor in concert as Petruchio kisses his wife's hand, present a perfect match. What's more, they have also "won the wager" (5.2.186).

As a final gesture, Fredi Olster's Kate throws a backwards glance at the live audience, whom she favors with a broad wink that signals her unimpaired high spirits. This direct wink into the camera—yet another meta-theatrical gesture aimed at softening the anti-feminist rhetoric of Kate's speech—was first performed on film in the 1929 *Taming of the Shrew*, although Mary Pickford's Kate directed her ironic signal to Bianca rather than to the film audience. Olster's wink, which solicits the viewer's complicity, balances Petruchio's soliloquy at the beginning of Act 4, where Petruchio directly challenges audience members to best him at shrew-taming, a move that elicits audible giggles from the filmed audience. At the end, Kate not only has the last word, but she achieves mastery by matching Petruchio word for word, gesture for gesture, move for move, speech for speech, and kiss for kiss.

WORKS CITED

Rothwell, Kenneth S., and Annabelle Henkin Melzer. *Shakespeare on Screen: An International Filmography and Videography*. New York and London: Neal-Schuman Publishers, Inc., 1990.

Rothwell, Kenneth, et al. "Production of *Taming of the Shrew.*" *SHAKSPER: The Global Electronic Shakespeare Conference*. 25 October, 2002. http://www.shaksper.net/archives/2002/2136.html (19 October, 2006).

Steele, Mike. "Theatre Wins Heart of San Francisco." *Minneapolis Tribune*, 5 May 1975.

Wilk, John R. *The Creation of an Ensemble: The First Years of the American Conservatory Theatre*. Carbondale, Ill.: Southern Illinois University Press, 1986.

The Taming of the Shrew. Director William Ball and Kirk Browning. Performers Marc Singer and Fredi Olster. Originally staged for the theater by The American Conservatory Theater of San Francisco. Presented by Thirteen/WNET, New York, Great Performances, Theatre in America, Educational Broadcasting System, 1976; DVD, Broadway Theatre Archive. Kultur, 2002.

"Kiss me, Kate"

THE TAMING OF THE SHREW IN POPULAR CULTURE

Douglas Lanier

"'TIS A WONDER, BY YOUR LEAVE, SHE WILL BE TAMED SO"

The Taming of the Shrew is one of several Shakespeare plays—*The Merchant of Venice, Othello, The Tempest*—whose content has become troubling to some modern spectators because of changes in social mores in the last century. After the advent of the feminist movement, it is difficult to portray Petruchio's shrew-taming unironically without provoking offense—or at least a wince—from modern audiences. It should be noted that in the context of other shrew-taming tales of the period, Shakespeare's approach to the subject seems unusual. Kate's shrewishness demonstrates sharp wit and intolerance of fools, qualities very much on display in her first exchange with Petruchio. Shakespeare also includes details that suggest that her aggressiveness springs from her secondary position in her father's favor as well as the humiliating nature of the marriage market, not simply from a woman's will to power. What's more, unlike most other Renaissance shrew-taming tales, Petruchio's approach to shrew-taming is psychological rather than physical; he beats his servants rather than his new wife, and he declares, however disingenuously, that he does all for the love of his wife. Most unusually, the tale of Kate and Petruchio is framed by an Induction that features a male shrew, Christopher Sly, Kate's seeming counterpart. The Induction might be taken to suggest that the play concerns the control of unruly characters, male or female through clever role-playing, rather than the domination of wives by their husbands.

Even so, whether the sharp edges of shrew-taming are really softened by these elements remains a matter for vigorous debate, particularly since modern spectators do not experience the play within its original context. There is some evidence that even in its own day, Shakespeare's *The Taming of the Shrew* was understood to be about power relations between husbands and wives. In the play's first sequel, John Fletcher's *The Woman's Prize, or The Tamer Tamed* (ca. 1611), Petruchio, now widowed, tries to repeat his taming regimen on his new wife, Maria. Fletcher turns the gender politics of wife-taming on their head when Maria organizes the women of the town

Lysistrata-style to resist male domination. This tale of a taming backfiring also surfaces 350 years later in "The Taming of Lucille," an episode of the classic TV sitcom *Car 54, Where Are You?* (aired December 3, 1961). Seeing a performance of *Shrew*, the ever dim-witted Officer Toody decides to tame his own wife Lucille using Shakespeare as his model. Ironically, the results are the reverse of what he desires, and eventually, he returns quite happily to his status as a hen-pecked husband. In rather interesting comic fashion, this TV show registers the gap between the outdated fantasy of male control that the play offers and the more complex realities of modern married life, all the while providing an amusing parody of Shakespeare.

Certainly there has been a longstanding theatrical tradition of treating Shakespeare's play as a tale of triumphal male bravado. One marker of that performance tradition is Petruchio's whip. Though mentioned nowhere in Shakespeare's script, it was a common prop for stage Petruchios throughout the eighteenth and nineteenth centuries. In fact, Petruchio's whip appears prominently in the first adaptation of the play to the talkies in 1929, only two years into the era of cinema sound. The adaptation was cleverly filmed so that it could play as both a talking and a silent picture, since many theaters did not yet have sound equipment installed. The film starred then-international screen stars Mary Pickford and Douglas Fairbanks, Jr. in a production that took advantage of the audience's knowledge that the two were married. (Famous husbands and wives were cast in the roles of Petruchio and Kate throughout the century: Alfred Lunt and Joan Fontaine are another famous example.) At the time of filming, Fairbanks had made a considerable name for himself playing a grinning swashbuckler, and so his whip-wielding, audacious Petruchio allowed him to exploit and parody his established screen persona, particularly one of his most famous silent roles, that of Zorro. An opening shot of a Punch and Judy show establishes from the start the slapstick war-of-the-sexes that dominates the film.

The match between established type and Shakespearean character was less felicitous for Mary Pickford, who had heretofore specialized in girlish—if occasionally feisty—heroines. At film's end, as Kate gives her final speech, Pickford seems to assume her familiar feminine meekness, but she ends her performance with a broad wink to the women, indicating her solidarity with feminist unruliness and a certain distance from her own screen persona. Unfortunately, the public didn't buy it, for the film was largely commercially unsuccessful, despite its considerable star power. Nonetheless, the film has its clever moments. Throughout the wedding scene, for example, Petruchio eats an apple; in the sound version, the echo of each crunchy bite makes for a terrific sound gag. The film was well-known enough to be parodied a year later in the British film *Elstree Calling* (1930). This musical and comedy revue ends with a parody of Petruchio and Kate's first encounter, which degenerates into a pie-throwing melee eventually involving Shakespeare himself.

THE *Shrew's* MANY SONGS

Later adaptations addressed the problematic nature of *Shrew*'s comedy in a variety of ways. Another bickering husband and wife team served as protagonists of one of the most successful musical adaptations of Shakespeare, *Kiss Me Kate* (1948). Taking its cue from Shakespeare's play-within-a-play, it cleverly adapts a tried and true storyline for musicals, a tale of a troupe's efforts to put on a musical show. In this case the show is a musical version of *The Taming of the Shrew*, and it is threatened by tensions between the leads Fred Graham and Lilli Vanessi, a showbiz team who, despite being divorced and involved with others, are still in love, though they cannot declare it outright. A number of features are noteworthy. Bianca is played as a coquette playing the romantic field, just as the actress playing Bianca is manipulating Graham's affections; a comic subplot involves Slug and Lippy, two goofy thugs fond of pompous language who eventually slip into the musical's onstage action. Slug and Lippy's "Brush up Your Shakespeare," a comically cynical song about using Shakespeare to woo women, is the show's most famous number and is typical of its clever self-consciousness. The musical's treatment of Petruchio's male bravado (and of Graham who plays the part) is equally wry. In George Sidney's 1953 film version, Petruchio reflects upon his past female conquests while lounging on a phallic pink wall, but he is soon revealed to be a chauvinist with feet of clay: despite his philandering, he still loves Lilli and is miserable when she leaves him and the show. In the end, Lilli returns and uses her performance of Kate's final speech to indicate her recognition that romantically and professionally, she and Graham are a match.

Though *Kiss Me, Kate* is by far the best-known musical adaptation of the play, it is not the only one. The 1944 film musical *Casanova in Burlesque* turns on issues of propriety which now seem quaint. The film tells the story of Shakespeare professor Joseph Kelly, who moonlights during his summer breaks as a vaudevillian at a burlesque house. When one of the strippers at the burlesque house finds out about his respectable identity, she threatens to expose his secret, forcing him to cast her as the lead in his production of *Romeo and Juliet*. When her bad acting ruins the show, the burlesque company improvises an unexpectedly successful swing version of *The*

Taming of the Shrew. One of the numbers is even entitled "Willie the Shake." John R. Briggs and Dennis West's 2000 musical *Romancin' the One I Love* uses the same backstage musical approach as *Kiss Me, Kate*, this time making Petruchio into a struggling dancer who marries Kate in an effort to make a quick buck; the show is distinguished less by its musical numbers than by its many allusions to screwball comedies of the 1930s. Operatic adaptations include Hermann Goetz's *Der Widerspenstigen Zahmung* (1874, libretto by Joseph Viktor Widmann) and Vittorio Giannini's *The Taming of the Shrew* (1953, with a libretto by Dorothy Fee that also includes passages from the sonnets and from *Romeo and Juliet*). Far more unusual is Ermanno Wolf-Ferrari's opera *Sly oder die Legende vom wiedererweckten Schläfer* (1927, aka *Sly, or the Legend of the Dreamer Reawakened*), which reimagines the play's induction as Sly's tragedy and has recently found a champion in the tenor superstar José Carreras. American composer Dominick Argento took a far more comic approach to the same source material in his chamber opera *Christopher Sly* (1962). Musical forms specific to national traditions have also been the basis for a handful of adaptations. Such is the case with J. Lopez Silva and Ruperto Chapí's *Las bravias* (1896), a *zarzuela* (Spanish musical burlesque) version of *The Taming of the Shrew*. More recently, in 2003 Hsing-lin Tracy Chung reworked Shakespeare's play for *jingju*, a traditional Chinese operatic form also known as "Beijing opera."

FRICTION AND ROMANCE

The notion that Petruchio is bluffing or only pretending to be domineering is another popular means for addressing the uncomfortable gender politics of the play. This is the approach of Franco Zeffirelli's film *The Taming of the Shrew* (1967), starring another famous screen couple, Richard Burton and Elizabeth Taylor. Like *Who's Afraid of Virginia Woolf* (1966), another Taylor-Burton film that features a bickering couple, Zeffirelli's *Shrew* exploits the audience's knowledge of the leads' tempestuous relationship and emphasizes their most famous assets—Burton's voice and Taylor's eyes.

The film announces its wry take on upper-class propriety by opening with a carnival in Padua in which established authority figures are mocked. The carnival theme runs throughout. Petruchio and Grumio arrive for the wedding with Kate dressed like characters from Brueghel's painting *The Battle of Carnival and Lent* (1559). Burton's Petruchio is all working-class bluff and bluster, indicated throughout the film by his comic boorishness and slightly nervous smile and laugh. At first Taylor's Kate seems an aristocratic harridan consumed by rage—her first encounter with Petruchio is an extended

Elizabeth Taylor as Kate and Richard Burton as Petruchio
in the 1967 Film directed by Franco Zeffirelli
© 1967 Columbia Pictures Corporation, Courtesy of Douglas Lanier

wrestling match and chase, hardly a war of words—yet despite her being brutalized by Petruchio, Kate quickly develops other means of exerting authority over her new husband, particularly through her housework at Petruchio's shabby home. Eventually Petruchio finds himself trapped by the domineering shrew-tamer role he has taken on, so much so that at the final wedding banquet the couple cannot express their obvious feelings for one another. His wager at the banquet is a huge, unsure gamble, and Kate uses the situation to chastise the insulting widow and to publicly declare her love for her genuinely surprised husband. That Kate's spirit is not crushed is underlined by the fact that she exits before Petruchio can complete his gloating. He is forced to run a gauntlet of spectators in pursuit of his wife, once again taking up the chase with which their relationship began.

As with *Much Ado About Nothing*, *The Taming of the Shrew* has served as more general inspiration for various tales of witty lovers whose bickering conceals an erotic attraction between them. This plotline is the stuff, for example, of many a Gothic romance novel, and homage to that Shakespearean legacy is paid in several examples with ties to *Shrew*, including Susan Carroll's *The Lady Who Hated Shakespeare* (1986), Helen Myers's *Kiss Me Kate* (1990), Eugenia Riley's *Taming Kate* (1992), Carla Kelly's *Miss*

Billings Treads the Boards (1993, in which the heroine plays the Widow), Joan Overfield's *A Proper Taming* (1994), Janet Bailey and Sonja Massie's "The Taming of Katherina" (1997, in *Unmasked*), and Elizabeth Bevarly's *My Man Pendleton* (1998, in which the protagonist is named "Kit"). Eloisa James's *The Taming of the Duke* (2006) reverses the gender of the shrew and in the process exemplifies an important way in which this plotline has been accommodated to a female readership's perspective: the tale of the bad boy conquered by the heroine's love.

The link between *Shrew* and the "bickering lovers" motif is also acknowledged in "Atomic Shakespeare," a much-beloved episode of the TV series *Moonlighting*, a comedy which featured two detectives, zany David Addison (played by Bruce Willis) and icy Maddie Hayes (played by Cybill Shepherd), who solved crimes while trading wisecracks and denying their mutual attraction. Like Shakespeare's play, this episode includes a comically self-referential induction in which a young boy, anxious to watch *Moonlighting*, is instead forced by his mother to do his Shakespeare homework instead of watching his favorite show. As the boy reads, we see his imagined version of Shakespeare's *Shrew*, with the major roles taken by series regulars (Willis as Petruchio, Shepherd as Katherine). Shakespeare's play and *Moonlighting* share features that this episode highlights with particular brilliance: lightning-quick repartee, pileups of puns, slapstick violence, direct address to the viewer, a plotline heavy on farce, courtship coupled with conflict, and self-mocking male bravado. Along the way, the episode frequently breaks frame to lampoon the characters' performances of Shakespeare, Elizabethan language, and period production, and to make silly allusions to various films and details from the series. When he arrives in Padua, Willis's Petruchio is a chauvinist wise-guy, a Renaissance version of his Addison character who plays the hip, bad boy with gusto and an ironic smirk. However, after their marriage, when Kate makes plain the erotic benefits of gender equality, Petruchio reveals his willingness to adopt a conciliatory, even tender relationship with her in private. Interestingly, Kate's climactic declaration of subjection is taken up by Petruchio in this adaptation. When Kate refuses to say that the sun is the moon, Petruchio publicly accedes to her better judgment and even refuses Baptista's dowry, offering his own version of Kate's speech: "For those with bodies soft and tender hath soft and tender hearts to match, and all their gifts be so much more, when allowed to be given freely. If this be offensive to men, so be it, as perhaps the time hath come for offense." However, whether or not this seeming triumph of modern feminism can be taken seriously is a matter of debate, for it allows for a darker reading, the pernicious myth that male chauvinism is really only an ironic mask for a heart of gold.

FANTASIES OF MALE POWER

Many popular references to and adaptations of *The Taming of the Shrew* suggest that for some the play remains a fantasy of male power, particularly in the face of challenges to that power throughout the twentieth century. It is striking, for example, the number of films made in the silent era's second decade which use variations on the title or plot of Shakespeare's play: *The Taming of Rita* (n.d.), *The Taming of the Shrew* (1908, directed by D. W. Griffiths), *The Taming of Jane* (1910), *The Taming of Mary* (1912), *The Taming of Betty* (1913), *The Taming of Mary* (1915), *The Iron Strain* (1915), *Taming Liza* (1916), *The Taming of Lucy* (1917), *Impossible Catherine* (1919), *The Indestructible Wife* (1919), and *Enchantment* (1921). Given that a woman's right to vote was granted in Britain in 1918 and the United States in 1920, such "taming of" films seem to speak to fears about women's growing independence and use Shakespeare's play as the basis for fantasies of putting women back in their "proper" place. In some cases, the woman's upper-class status also fuels her independence, so that taming her also becomes a populist fantasy of defeating the social elite. This fantasy has its own long legacy, seen in, for example, Lina Wertmüller's controversial film *Swept Away* (aka *Travolti da un insolito destino nell'azzurro mare d'agosto*, 1974), in which a working-class sailor tames and seduces an arrogant socialite when the two become marooned on a desert island. The TV series *Quantum Leap* featured a mild-for-TV adaptation of a similar story ("Leaping of the Shrew," aired 29 September 1992), and a recent, much-maligned remake of Wertmüller's film (2002, dir. Guy Ritchie) starred Madonna in the lead role. Somewhat related to this group is "Elaan of Troyius," an installment of the original *Star Trek* series (aired 25 November 1986), in which Captain Kirk attempts to tame a bratty alien princess who is an intergalactic treaty bride. Though the two fall in love, Kirk's duty to his ship and Elaan's duty to her people eventually triumph.

WESTERN AND HISPANIC VERSIONS

The "taming of" films of the silent era are matched by a series of "taming of the men" films during the same period—*Taming a Husband* (1909 and 1910), *Taming a Grandfather* (1910), *The Taming of Buck* (1910), *The Taming of Big Ben* (1912), *The Taming of Texas Pete* (1913), *Taming a Tenderfoot* (1913), and *The Taming of Grouchy Bill* (1916), the last three of which cowboy actor Tom

Mix was the star. The analogy between taming an unruly woman (or man) and taming uncivilized territory, hinted at in Mix's "taming" films, has prompted a long-standing relationship between Shakespeare's play and the genre of the Western, a connection explored in various examples:

WESTERN ADAPTATIONS OF *THE TAMING OF THE SHREW*	
McLintock! (1963)	John Wayne as George Washington McLintock tames his ex-wife Katherine played by Maureen O'Hara
"The Wooing of Perilous Pauline," (aired 7, January 1964)	an episode of the TV series *Death Valley Days*
"Woman of Fire," (aired 17, January 1965)	an episode of the TV series *Bonanza*
Chief Shaking Spear Rides Again (or the Taming of the Sioux) (1975)	Warren Graves's western themed play adapted from Shakespeare's *The Taming of the Shrew*
Bronco Billy (1980)	Clint Eastwood as Bronco Billy, proprietor-manager of a rag-tag Wild West show, tames Antoinette, a bitchy socialite
The Taming of the Shrew, Shakespeare in the Park, 1990	a much-acclaimed Western-themed 1990 performance of the play for New York City's Shakespeare in the Park which starred Tracey Ullmann and Morgan Freeman

Of this group, *McLintock!* is of special interest, since it stars John Wayne, a star so closely identified with the Western hero, at a moment where his popularity had somewhat waned. In the film, Wayne's character *McLintock*, a gruff rancher, finds himself at the end of the heroic era of Western expansion, beset on all sides by government bureaucrats, arriving homesteaders, the values of the citified East, and overly prim women. Since he cannot fight the encroachment of "civilization," his response is the symbolic one, that of taming his boisterous, society-conscious ex-wife, giving her a public spanking and winning her heart. In the process, *McLintock* teaches local farmhand

Dev how to treat his new wife, *McLintock*'s own daughter Rebecca. *McLintock!* sought to capitalize upon Wayne and O'Hara's chemistry from the commercially successful *The Quiet Man* (1952), where the two also played a comically bickering couple. Indeed, many commentators have detected distant resemblances between *The Quiet Man* and *The Taming of the Shrew*.

Maureen O'Hara and John Wayne in the film *McLintock!* (1963)
Photo Courtesy of Douglas Lanier

Several classics of Mexican cinema offer variations on the motif of the cowboy tamer, resituating stories of a fiery courtship on haciendas or rural territories and emphasizing the *machismo* of the tamer as well as the fiery sensuality of the shrew. All draw as much (or more) upon traditional Spanish shrew-taming tales as they do on Shakespeare's play. Examples include: *Enamorada* (1946, set during the Mexican revolution), *Cartas Marcadas* (1948), *El Charro y La Dama* (1949, a film which particularly emphasizes the class differences between tamer and shrew), *El Rapto* (1954), the sequence "La tigresa" in *Canasta de Cuentos Mexicanos* (1956), and *Más fuerte que el amor* (1959). Though not Mexican and not situated in a rural setting, the Brazilian soap opera *O Cravo e a Rosa* (2000), centered around the romantic tensions between Catherine Batista and Julião Petruchio, testifies to the continuing vitality of *Shrew* and its analogues with Latin American audiences.

The link between Shakespeare's play and traditional Latin *machismo* also figures in the film *La fierecilla domada* (1956), directed by the eminent Spanish filmmaker Antonio Román. Set in the nineteenth century, this version stars Carmen Sevilla, noted Spanish film star and singer, in the role of the fearsome Catalina; her provocatively mannish independence is made clear when she first enters the film wearing a man's clothing and a sword and swaggering on horseback. Other European cinemas also include adaptations influenced (albeit distantly) by *The Taming of the Shrew*. A relatively faithful Italian film version was directed by Ferdinando Maria Poggioli in 1942. *Kohlhiesels Töchter* (1920, aka *Kohlhiesel's Daughters*), directed by the great German comic director Ernst Lubitsch, tells the tale of Bavarian innkeeper Mathias Kohlhiesel's two daughters, the younger coquette Greta and her older sister, the hellion Liesel. To get around the father's declaration that the younger cannot be courted until the latter is married, Peter resolves to marry then divorce Liesel so he can have Greta, but in the process of taming Liesel he falls in love with her. A considerable hit at the box office, this film was remade three times, each time with the same casting gimmick–the two sisters are played by the same actress. Two Hungarian films, *Makacs Kata* and *Makrancos hölgy*, both made in 1943 by different studios, offer tales of headstrong city wives being tamed by their husbands of traditional peasant stock. The opposition between city women and country men in these films, Louise O. Vasvári has argued, speaks to anxieties about the erosion of traditional peasant culture, an important touchstone of Hungarian identity, in the modern era.

"SEE HIM DRESSED IN ALL SUITS LIKE A LADY": TOYING WITH GENDER

Yet another means of addressing the problematic sexual politics of Shakespeare's play is to scramble the gender identifications of his characters, rendering the man the shrew and the woman the tamer and thereby rendering the male-female power relations all the more visible and farcical. This is the strategy of a handful of recent productions of *The Taming of the Shrew*, including Kenneth Nowell's 1997 production for New York City's Looking Glass Theater and Harry Teplitz's *Kiss Me, Nate* (1999) for the Rose Alley Theater in Los Angeles (with Katherine as "Nathaniel" and Petruchio as "Patricia"). A version of the same approach can be found in the French film

L'ours et la Poupee (1970, aka *The Bear and the Doll*), starring the then fading star Brigitte Bardot. In this farce, a reclusive musician Gaspard meets Felicia, a Parisian model, when her car breaks down near his country home. When Gaspard treats Felicia with unaccustomed disinterest, she becomes determined to break through his romantic "shrewishness." Obviously, no small appeal of the film is the male fantasy of being pursued by a liberated, aggressive, beautiful woman, and once again, the scenario plays upon the familiar contrast between the sexually liberated world of the city woman and the traditional realm of the rural man. A similar plot underlies the Italian film farce *Il Bisbetico domato* (aka *The Taming of the Scoundrel*), made ten years later. In this version, the beautiful woman eventually gives up her pursuit and the rural man, soon regretful at losing her, wins her back with a spectacular public declaration of his love at a sports game.

Single-gender productions of the play have also been mounted, including an all-women performance in 2005 by the Queen's Company in New York City (with the part of Bianca played by an inflatable doll) and an all-male performance in 2007 by the Propeller Company at the Old Vic in London. In their stagings of Kate's final speech, the Queen's Company emphasizes Kate's indominability, while Propeller stresses Petruchio's brutality and Kate's disturbingly exhausted submission. Clayton Kinnelon Greiman takes single-gender production one step further in his *Kiss Me, Nate (Or Why Boys Are The Biggest Bitches of All)*, a 2002 play which reimagines Shakespeare's play as a camped-up gay farce. In this version, *shrew*ish Nate remains untamed and miserable until the end, and it is Lucentio and Gabriel who end the play with a kiss. Three altogether different film adaptations—pornographic—have been produced since 1997, one of which offers a quite literalistic version of Kate and Petruchio's bawdy puns in their first meeting. Though these adaptations testify to the extraordinary cultural reach of Shakespeare's comedy, they also work to reinstate the very subordination of women to men that recent productions have so often labored to question.

TAMING THE MODERN FEMINIST SHREW IN *10 THINGS I HATE ABOUT YOU* AND *DELIVER US FROM EVA*

Two recent film adaptations of *The Taming of the Shrew* suggest how the play has been transformed to fit the contemporary world and the demands of youth-oriented romantic comedy. Both films reconceive of Kate as a young modern-day feminist (of sorts) who must struggle to reconcile her fiercely-held independence with her desire for romance. In the tradition of 90s teen Shakespeare, *10 Things I Hate About You* resituates the play in an American high school stratified into various social cliques. The plot is set in motion by the efforts of Cameron to court Bianca, whose overprotective father makes her dating life contingent upon her *shrew*ish feminist sister Kat first getting a date. Cameron hires bad-boy Patrick to woo Kat and soon Patrick and Kat find themselves enjoying each other's rebellious streaks, but when Kat discovers that Patrick has been hired to date her, their romance temporarily founders. Beneath this conventional tale of boy-meets-girl, boy-loses-girl, boy-regains-girl's-trust is a contradictory engagement with 90s grrl power. Kat's caustic but witty feminism springs, we learn, not from political commitment but from romantic disillusionment, and so by the logic of teen romance her character must move from altogether rejecting men (early in the film Kat goes to an all-girl night club where Patrick meets her) to finding an accommodation between her feminist nature and romance. That accommodation comes at the end of the film when Patrick gives her a guitar to regain her love. Whether or not that guitar–a symbol of the grrl bands Kat likes and, by extension, grrl power itself–signifies Patrick's genuine appreciation of Kat's independent nature or is merely a superficial bribe for her forgiveness is a matter for debate. In fact, when Kat protests a bit at Patrick's gesture, Patrick stops her speech with a kiss, an action that might be seen as romantic or controlling. Also noteworthy is the film's divided attitude toward citation of Shakespeare. Several direct quotations appear–from the romantically naive Cameron and from a witty English teacher–and the romantic qualities of Shakespeare even form the basis for a courtship between two nerds in a comic subplot, but Patrick makes clear that he finds Shakespearean quotation very uncool, even though ironically he is the protagonist in a Shakespeare movie.

A second, equally interesting film adaptation of *Shrew* is the aptly-titled *Deliver Us From Eva*, an African-American romantic comedy starring rapper LL Cool J and Gabrielle Union (who also appears in *10 Things*). In *Deliver* the shrew is Eva, a sharp-tongued professional woman who rules over the lives of her three younger sisters, much to their husbands' and boyfriends' irritation. The men hire Ray, a notorious "master player," to woo and dump Eva so she will no longer interfere in their relationships, but after initial sparks Ray and Eva fall for each other and become serious, threatening their plan. Like Kat in *10 Things*, Eva is a feminist with a troubled romantic past, but her feminism springs from her concern to insure her sisters' personal and professional success in the wake of the women's difficult upbringing. The film weds Shakespeare's *Shrew* with African-American traditions of strong maternal figures and the threat of the "love 'em and leave 'em" lothario; in an interesting twist, in the course of the plot Ray becomes tamed perhaps far more than is Eva. Equally interesting are differences in social class between Ray and Eva that at first provide a source of tension. While Eva is a professional city restaurant inspector, Ray is a working-class meat packer who early on shows up for a date with Eva with his delivery truck. The class differences faintly harken to the city-country dichotomy between female shrew and male tamer so apparent in many popular adaptations, though the film quickly reveals that Ray has elite connections and middle-class ambitions. Eventually the storyline descends into farce. The men attempt to fake Ray's death to enable Eva to take an out-of-town job, and Ray reveals to Eva the deal to date her for cash. In an ending reminiscent of the final scene of *10 Things*, Ray mends the relationship by giving Eva a gift, in her case a horse, symbolic of Eva's childhood ambition to become a horse trainer before disaster struck her family. In a deviation from Shakespeare's play, it is Ray who delivers the long final speech declaring his devotion to Eva, and it is Eva who takes the reins as the two ride off on the white steed.

These two films suggest that despite *The Taming of the Shrew*'s seemingly outdated conception of gender relations, popular culture has found ways to use the play even to address contemporary feminism, though not always without compromising its political ideals. It is productive to understand popular adaptations of *Shrew* as responses to anxieties and assumptions about women's growing power and men's losses of privilege in the modern world. Because those anxieties remain very much in play as women's status continues to change, it is likely that *The Taming of the Shrew* will continue to remain one of popular culture's more durable Shakespearean touchstones.

Dramatis Personae

INDUCTION:
A Lord
Christopher Sly, a tinker
Hostess
Page, Huntsmen, Servants, Players

THE TAMING OF THE SHREW:
Baptista Minola of Padua
Katherina, the shrew, elder daughter of Baptista
Bianca, younger daughter of Baptista
Vincentio, a merchant of Pisa
Lucentio, son to Vincentio, in love with Bianca
Petruchio, a gentleman of Verona, a suitor to Katherina
Gremio, suitor to Bianca
Hortensio, suitor to Bianca
Tranio, servant to Lucentio
Biondello, servant to Lucentio
Grumio, servant to Petruchio
Curtis, servant to Petruchio
A Pedant
A Widow
Tailor
Haberdasher
Servants attending on Baptista and Petruchio
Nathaniel
Philip
Joseph
Nicholas
Peter

[The Taming of the Shrew
Induction

0: Scene: One of the first questions before any production of *Shrew* is whether the Inductions will be included. The two most widely seen filmed productions, Zeffirelli's (1966) and Jonathan Miller's BBC (1980), do not include them; Henry Fenwick's account of the production prefacing the BBC Shakespeare text of the play says that this was done to help "the seriousness of the approach." Of the six Royal Shakespeare Company productions between 1982 and 2003, four included some version of the inductions, sometimes with few of the original words, and two, including another directed by Jonathan Miller, did not. The habit of substituting or adding modern dialogue to the inductions is quite widespread: the 2007 American Shakespeare Center touring production of the play does this, with Sly entering through the audience, shouting drunken complaints. Barry Kyle's 1982 RSC production began with a noisy, prolonged alehouse scene, with dancing and inarticulate shouting that finally became the Sly/Hostess argument. In Bill Alexander's 1992 RSC production, the Sly frame was in place, in modern dress. In Lindsay Posner's 1999 RSC production, the Inductions, unlike the rest of the play, were in modern dress with the Lord and the huntsmen in hunting pink.

1: Speech Prefix: **SLY**: The First Folio reads *"Begger"* here and *"Beg."* in subsequent lines throughout the inductions; Rowe (1709) emended these prefixes to Sly, and we follow suit.
1: **feeze you**: fix you, do for you; possibly beat or flog
2: **A pair of stocks**: I'll have you put in the stocks
3: **baggage**: worthless, good-for-nothing woman; woman of disreputable or immoral life, strumpet; **Chronicles**: historical chronicles such as Raphael Holinshed's (1577) used by Shakespeare
4: **Richard Conqueror**: mistake for William the Conqueror, who conquered England in 1066
3-4: Scene: **the Slys...Conqueror**: Penny Gay reports (in "Recent Australian Shrews") that in Aubrey Mellor's Queensland Theatre Company production in 1989 Sly followed "rogues" with "We came with the First Fleet," equivalent to an American saying "We came with the Mayflower" but making an additional point since most of those who arrived in Australia with the First Fleet were convicts.
4: *paucas pallabris*: few words (incorrect version of the Spanish *"pocas palabras"*)
5: **Sessa**: meaning not certain, but appears to be "be quiet" or "stop it"
7: **denier**: small copper coin (used to denote a very small sum); **Saint Jeronimy**: St. Jerome
9: **thirdborough**: petty constable of a town or manor. The First Folio's "Headborough" means the same but as Theobald first pointed out in 1726, Sly's joke (Induction 1.10) makes less sense without the emendation.
11: **kindly**: welcome (meant sarcastically)
12: **tender well**: take good care of
13: **Breathe Merriman**: i.e., Let Merriman catch his breath. The First Folio reads "Brach" (i.e., bitch), but C. J. Sisson argued in 1956 for the emendation to "breathe"; **embossed**: foaming at the mouth
14: **deep-mouthed brach**: deep-voiced bitch

Induction, Scene 1]

Enter [CHRISTOPHER SLY] and HOSTESS

SLY
  I'll feeze you, in faith

HOSTESS
  A pair of stocks, you rogue!

SLY
  Y'are a baggage; the Slys are no rogues. Look in the Chronicles;
  we came in with Richard Conqueror. Therefore *paucas pallabris*,
  let the world slide. Sessa!   5

HOSTESS
  You will not pay for the glasses you have burst?

SLY
  No, not a denier. Go by, Saint Jeronimy, go to thy cold bed, and
  warm thee.

HOSTESS
  I know my remedy, I must go fetch the thirdborough.

                                                              [Exit]

SLY
  Third, or fourth, or fifth borough, I'll answer him by law. I'll not   10
  budge an inch, boy. Let him come, and kindly.
                                       Falls asleep.Wind horns.
                          Enter a LORD from hunting, with his train.

LORD
  Huntsman, I charge thee, tender well my hounds.
  Breathe Merriman—the poor cur is embossed—
  And couple Clowder with the deep-mouthed brach,

15: **made it good**: picked up the scent

16: **in the coldest fault**: when the scent had gone completely cold

19: **at the merest loss**: when the scent was entirely lost

24: **sup them well**: give them a good supper

31: **Grim death...thine image**: The image or likeness of death is sleep.

32: **practice on**: play a trick on

34: **sweet**: perfumed

36: **brave**: well dressed

38: **cannot choose**: cannot help doing it; is bound to do it

Saw'st thou not, boy, how Silver made it good 15
At the hedge corner, in the coldest fault?
I would not lose the dog for twenty pound.

FIRST HUNTSMAN
Why, Belman is as good as he, my Lord.
He cried upon it at the merest loss,
And twice to day picked out the dullest scent. 20
Trust me, I take him for the better dog.

LORD
Thou art a fool. If Echo were as fleet,
I would esteem him worth a dozen such.
But sup them well, and look unto them all.
Tomorrow I intend to hunt again. 25

FIRST HUNTSMAN
I will, my lord.

LORD
What's here? One dead, or drunk? See, doth he breathe?

SECOND HUNTSMAN
He breathes, my lord. Were he not warmed with ale,
This were a bed but cold to sleep so soundly.

LORD
Oh monstrous beast, how like a swine he lies! 30
Grim death, how foul and loathsome is thine image!
Sirs, I will practice on this drunken man.
What think you, if he were conveyed to bed,
Wrapped in sweet clothes, rings put upon his fingers,
A most delicious banquet by his bed, 35
And brave attendants near him when he wakes,
Would not the beggar then forget himself?

FIRST HUNTSMAN
Believe me, lord, I think he cannot choose.

40: **flattering**: pleasing; **fancy**: fantasy

42: **fairest**: most beautiful

43: **wanton**: sexual, lewd, self-indulgent, luxurious

44: **balm**: wash, bathe; **foul**: disgusting, smelly

47: **dulcet**: melodious

48: **straight**: immediately

49: **reverence**: bow

53: **ewer**: jug; **diaper**: towel

60: **when he says he is**: when he says he must be mad

62: **kindly**: naturally, so that it will be convincing

64: **husbanded with modesty**: managed carefully or with restraint

66: **As**: so that; **by**: as a result of

68-69: "Take him up gently, and to bed with him, / And each one to his office when he wakes": Max Wright as Christopher Sly, Ramon Deocampo as Lord and cast member in the 1999 Joseph Papp Public Theater production directed by Mel Shapiro
Photo: Michal Daniel

69: Stage Direction: *[SLY is carried off]*: not in the First Folio; Lewis Theobald (1733) emends with "*Some bear out Sly*"

70: **Sirrah**: term of address used to inferiors

SECOND HUNTSMAN
    It would seem strange unto him when he waked.

LORD
    Even as a flattering dream, or worthless fancy.   40
    Then take him up, and manage well the jest.
    Carry him gently to my fairest chamber,
    And hang it round with all my wanton pictures;
    Balm his foul head in warm distillèd waters,
    And burn sweet wood to make the lodging sweet;   45
    Procure me music ready when he wakes,
    To make a dulcet and a heavenly sound;
    And if he chance to speak, be ready straight
    And with a low submissive reverence
    Say, "What is it your Honor will command?"   50
    Let one attend him with a silver basin
    Full of rose-water, and bestrewed with flowers,
    Another bear the ewer, the third a diaper,
    And say "Will't please your lordship cool your hands?"
    Some one be ready with a costly suit,   55
    And ask him what apparel he will wear.
    Another tell him of his hounds and horse,
    And that his lady mourns at his disease.
    Persuade him that he hath been lunatic,
    And when he says he is, say that he dreams,   60
    For he is nothing but a mighty lord.
    This do, and do it kindly, gentle sirs,
    It will be pastime passing excellent,
    If it be husbanded with modesty.

FIRST HUNTSMAN
    My lord, I warrant you we will play our part   65
    As he shall think by our true diligence
    He is no less than what we say he is.

LORD
    Take him up gently, and to bed with him,
    And each one to his office when he wakes.
                        [SLY is carried off.] Sound trumpets.
    Sirrah, go see what trumpet 'tis that sounds.   70

70: Stage Direction: *[Exit SERVINGMAN]*: not in the First Folio; emendation first made by Theobald (1733) to "*Ex. Servant*"

71: **Belike**: perhaps, probably

73: **An't**: if it

78: Speech Prefix: **FIRST PLAYER**: the First Folio reads "*2. Player*" but since this is the first player to speak individually, we follow G. R. Hibbard's emendation (1968) in assigning this speech.

78: **So please**: if it please; **duty**: respect, conduct due to a superior

84: Speech Prefix: **SECOND PLAYER**: the First Folio reads "*Sincklo*" (for John Sincklo or Sincler, an actor with the King's Men); emendation first made by Brian Morris (1981)

86: **in happy time**: at the right time

87: **The rather for**: especially because

88: **cunning**: skill

[Exit SERVINGMAN]

Belike some noble gentleman that means,
Traveling some journey, to repose him here.

Enter SERVINGMAN

How now? Who is it?

SERVINGMAN
                    An't please your honor, players
That offer service to your Lordship.

LORD
Bid them come near.

Enter PLAYERS

                    Now, fellows, you are welcome.   75

PLAYERS
We thank your honor.

LORD
Do you intend to stay with me tonight?

FIRST PLAYER
So please your Lordship to accept our duty.

LORD
With all my heart. This fellow I remember,
Since once he played a farmer's eldest son —   80
'Twas where you wooed the gentlewoman so well—
I have forgot your name, but sure that part
Was aptly fitted, and naturally performed.

SECOND PLAYER
I think 'twas Soto that your honor means.

LORD
'Tis very true, thou didst it excellent.   85
Well, you are come to me in happy time,
The rather for I have some sport in hand
Wherein your cunning can assist me much.
There is a lord will hear you play tonight;

90: **modesties**: self-control

91: **over-eyeing**: seeing, noticing

96: Speech Prefix: **FIRST PLAYER**: the First Folio reads "*Plai.*"; Edward Capell emended(1768) to "*1. P*"

97: **veriest antic**: oddest person, eccentric buffoon

98: **buttery**: pantry or kitchen storeroom. As Pope pointed out in his 1728 Preface, "meer players" would of course be "led into the Buttery by the Steward, not plac'd at the Lord's table".

100: **want**: lack, have want for; **affords**: can provide

102: **in all suits**: in every detail

104: **do him obeisance**: show him respect (as to a superior)

105: **as he will**: if he wants to

110: **tongue**: voice; **courtesy**: curtsey

118: **esteemèd him**: considered himself

122: **shift**: purpose, stratagem

But I am doubtful of your modesties,   90
Lest over-eyeing of his odd behavior,
(For yet his honor never heard a play)
You break into some merry passion,
And so offend him; for I tell you, sirs,
If you should smile, he grows impatient.   95

FIRST PLAYER
Fear not, my lord, we can contain ourselves,
Were he the veriest antic in the world.

LORD
Go, sirrah, take them to the buttery,
And give them friendly welcome every one.
Let them want nothing that my house affords.   100
Exit one with the PLAYERS

Sirrah, go you to Barthol'mew my page,
And see him dressed in all suits like a lady.
That done, conduct him to the drunkard's chamber,
And call him "Madam," do him obeisance.
Tell him from me, as he will win my love,   105
He bear himself with honorable action,
Such as he hath observed in noble ladies
Unto their lords, by them accomplishèd.
Such duty to the drunkard let him do
With soft low tongue, and lowly courtesy,   110
And say, "What is't your honor will command,
Wherein your lady, and your humble wife,
May show her duty, and make known her love?"
And then with kind embracements, tempting kisses,
And with declining head into his bosom,   115
Bid him shed tears, as being over-joyed
To see her noble lord restored to health,
Who for this seven years hath esteemèd him
No better than a poor and loathsome beggar.
And if the boy have not a woman's gift   120
To rain a shower of commanded tears,
An onion will do well for such a shift,
Which in a napkin being close conveyed

124: **in despite**: in spite (of a natural wish to laugh)

126: **Anon**: soon, shortly

127: **usurp**: take on, assume

128: **gait**: stride

130: **stay**: keep

132: **I'll in**: I'll go in; **Haply**: perhaps

133: **abate**: lessen; **spleen**: mood (in this case, the impulse to laugh)

Shall in despite enforce a watery eye.
See this dispatched with all the haste thou canst;   125
Anon I'll give thee more instructions.

                                             Exit a SERVINGMAN

I know the boy will well usurp the grace,
Voice, gait, and action of a gentlewoman.
I long to hear him call the drunkard "Husband,"
And how my men will stay themselves from laughter   130
When they do homage to this simple peasant,
I'll in to counsel them. Haply my presence
May well abate the over-merry spleen,
Which otherwise would grow into extremes.

                                             [Exeunt]

o: no scene division in the First Folio; Capell (1768) first made this division

o: Stage Direction: *[SLY]*: the First Folio reads "*the drunkard*"; we follow Rowe's emendation (1709) here and throughout the scene

1: "For God's sake, a pot of small ale": Max Wright as Christopher Sly and Ensemble in the 1999 Joseph Papp Public Theater production directed by Mel Shapiro
Photo: Michal Daniel

1: **small**: weak and cheap
2: **Lordship**: the First Folio reads "*Lord* "; this emendation first made in the 1631 quarto; **sack**: a kind of imported white wine
3: **conserves**: candied fruits
4: **raiment**: clothing
7: **conserves of beef**: stores of salted meat; also a pun on candied conserves (I.2.3)
8: **doublets**: close-fitting jackets
17: **cardmaker**: maker of cards for combing wool; **bear-herd**: keeper of a tame performing bear
18: **tinker**: pot mender; **alewife**: woman who keeps an alehouse
19–20: **on the score**: in debt
20: **sheer**: nothing but; **score me up for**: think of me as
21: **bestraught**: distraught, distracted, crazy

Induction, Scene 2]

Enter aloft [SLY] with attendants, some with apparel,
basin and ewer, and other appurtenances, and LORD

SLY
For God's sake, a pot of small ale.

FIRST SERVINGMAN
Will't please your Lordship drink a cup of sack?

SECOND SERVINGMAN
Will't please your honor taste of these conserves?

THIRD SERVINGMAN
What raiment will your honor wear today?

SLY
I am Christophero Sly, call not me "honor" nor "lordship." I ne'er   5
drank sack in my life, and if you give me any conserves, give me
conserves of beef. Ne'er ask me what raiment I'll wear, for I have
no more doublets than backs, no more stockings than legs, nor no
more shoes than feet—nay, sometime more feet than shoes, or
such shoes as my toes look through the over-leather.   10

LORD
Heaven cease this idle humor in your honor.
Oh that a mighty man of such descent,
Of such possessions, and so high esteem,
Should be infusèd with so foul a spirit.

SLY
What, would you make me mad? Am not I Christopher Sly, old   15
Sly's son of Burton-heath, by birth a pedlar, by education a
cardmaker, by transmutation a bear-herd, and now by present
profession a tinker? Ask Marian Hacket, the fat alewife of
Wincot, if she know me not. If she say I am not fourteen pence on
the score for sheer ale, score me up for the lyingest knave in   20
Christendom. What, I am not bestraught; here's—

23: **droop**: slouch, lose spirit

25: **As**: as if

27: **ancient**: former

30: **office**: employment, position; **beck**: nod, command

31: **Hark**: listen, hearken; **Apollo**: god of music, here (also the god of poetry, healing arts, archery and prophecy)

34–35: **the lustful...Semiramis**: Queen of Assyria, known for her looks and for her sexual adventures

36: **bestrew**: scatter or cover

37: **trapped**: adorned

41: **welkin**: sky

43: **course**: hunt hares with hounds

44: **breathèd**: good-winded; **roe**: small deer

46: **Adonis**: According to classical mythology, Adonis was a beautiful youth with whom Venus (here Cytherea) fell in love; here he is bathing in a brook while Cytherea hides in the grasses and spies on him.

48: **wanton**: play or move amorously

THIRD SERVINGMAN
Oh, this it is that makes your lady mourn.

SECOND SERVINGMAN
Oh, this is it that makes your servants droop.

LORD
Hence comes it that your kindred shuns your house
As beaten hence by your strange lunacy.   25
Oh noble lord, bethink thee of thy birth,
Call home thy ancient thoughts from banishment,
And banish hence these abject lowly dreams.
Look how thy servants do attend on thee,
Each in his office ready at thy beck.   30
Wilt thou have music? Hark, Apollo plays,
And twenty cagèd nightingales do sing.

Music

Or wilt thou sleep? We'll have thee to a couch,
Softer and sweeter than the lustful bed
On purpose trimmed up for Semiramis.   35
Say thou wilt walk; we will bestrew the ground.
Or wilt thou ride? Thy horses shall be trapped,
Their harness studded all with gold and pearl.
Dost thou love hawking? Thou hast hawks will soar
Above the morning lark. Or wilt thou hunt?   40
Thy hounds shall make the welkin answer them
And fetch shrill echoes from the hollow earth.

FIRST SERVINGMAN
Say thou wilt course, thy greyhounds are as swift
As breathèd stags, ay, fleeter than the roe.

SECOND SERVINGMAN
Dost thou love pictures? We will fetch thee straight   45
Adonis painted by a running brook,
And Cytherea all in sedges hid,
Which seem to move and wanton with her breath,
Even as the waving sedges play with wind.

50: **Io**: priestess of Juno with whom Jupiter fell in love; he concealed himself in a mist and raped her, after which she was turned into a heifer; **maid**: virgin

53: **Daphne**: In classical mythology, Daphne was pursued by Apollo and begged for help to get away from him; she escaped by being changed into a laurel tree.

56: **workmanly**: skilfully, expertly

59: **waning**: declining, deteriorating

64: "Am I a lord, and have I such a lady?": Jonathan Pryce as Christopher Sly and Ensemble in the 1978 Royal Shakespeare Company production directed by Michael Bogdanov
Photo: Donald Cooper

LORD
> We'll shew thee Io as she was a maid,   50
> And how she was beguilèd and surprised,
> As lively painted, as the deed was done.

THIRD SERVINGMAN
> Or Daphne roaming through a thorny wood,
> Scratching her legs that one shall swear she bleeds,
> And at that sight shall sad Apollo weep,   55
> So workmanly the blood and tears are drawn.

LORD
> Thou art a lord, and nothing but a lord.
> Thou hast a lady far more beautiful
> Than any woman in this waning age.

FIRST SERVINGMAN
> And till the tears that she hath shed for thee   60
> Like envious floods o'er-run her lovely face,
> She was the fairest creature in the world,
> And yet she is inferior to none.

SLY
> Am I a lord, and have I such a lady?
> Or do I dream? Or have I dreamed till now?   65
> I do not sleep: I see, I hear, I speak,
> I smell sweet savors, and I feel soft things.
> Upon my life, I am a lord indeed,
> And not a tinker, nor Christopher Sly.
> Well, bring our lady hither to our sight,   70
> And once again a pot o' th' smallest ale.

SECOND SERVINGMAN
> Will't please your mightiness to wash your hands?
> Oh, how we joy to see your wit restored;
> Oh, that once more you knew but what you are!
> These fifteen years you have been in a dream,   75
> Or when you waked, so waked as if you slept.

77: **fay**: faith; **goodly**: fine, substantial

78: **of**: in

79: **idle**: silly, meaningless

81: **beaten out of door**: turned out of the house

82: **rail upon**: complain bitterly about, strongly denounce; **house**: alehouse, tavern

83: **leet**: manorial court

84: **sealed quarts**: quart containers officially sealed and therefore guaranteed to contain the correct amount (implying the "stone jugs" contain less than one quart)

88: **reckoned up**: enumerated, listed

93: **amends**: recovery

94: Speech Prefix: **PAGE**: the First Folio reads "*Lady* " and "*La.*"; emendation first made by Capell (1768)

96: **fares**: Here "fares" refers to Sly's health; in the next line Sly uses "fare" to refer to drink and food.

97: **Marry**: in truth, to be sure (an oath derived from the name of the Virgin Mary)

SLY

These fifteen years! By my fay, a goodly nap,
But did I never speak of all that time?

FIRST SERVINGMAN

Oh yes, my lord, but very idle words,
For though you lay here in this goodly chamber,   80
Yet would you say ye were beaten out of door,
And rail upon the hostess of the house,
And say you would present her at the leet,
Because she brought stone jugs, and no sealed quarts.
Sometimes you would call out for Cicely Hacket.   85

SLY

Ay, the woman's maid of the house.

THIRD SERVINGMAN

Why, sir, you know no house, nor no such maid,
Nor no such men as you have reckoned up,
As Stephen Sly, and old John Naps of Greece,
And Peter Turph, and Henry Pimpernell,   90
And twenty more such names and men as these,
Which never were, nor no man ever saw.

SLY

Now Lord be thankèd for my good amends.

ALL

Amen.

Enter [the PAGE as a] LADY with ATTENDANTS

SLY

I thank thee, thou shalt not lose by it.   95

PAGE

How fares my noble lord?

SLY

Marry I, fare well, for here is cheer enough.
Where is my wife?

99: "Here, noble lord, what is thy will with her?": Jonathan Epstein as Sly with cast member in the Shakespeare Theatre Company's 1994-1995 production directed by Adrian Hall
Photo: Carol Pratt

101: **goodman**: lower-class term for husband

112: Stage Direction: *[Exeunt Servingmen]*: Not in the First Folio, Sir Arthur Quiller-Couch and John Dover Wilson emended to "the servants withdraw" in 1928

PAGE
    Here, noble lord, what is thy will with her?

SLY
    Are you my wife, and will not call me husband?   100
    My men should call me "lord"; I am your goodman.

PAGE
    My husband and my lord, my lord and husband,
    I am your wife in all obedience.

SLY
    I know it well; what must I call her?

LORD
    "Madam."   105

SLY
    "Al'ce Madam," or "Joan Madam"?

LORD
    "Madam" and nothing else, so lords call ladies.

SLY
    Madam wife, they say that I have dreamed
    And slept above some fifteen year or more.

PAGE
    Ay, and the time seems thirty unto me,   110
    Being all this time abandoned from your bed.

SLY
    'Tis much. Servants, leave me and her alone.

                                                    [Exeunt Servingmen]

    Madam, undress you, and come now to bed.

PAGE
    Thrice noble lord, let me entreat of you
    To pardon me yet for a night or two,   115

118: **In peril...malady**: in danger of relapsing with the former illness

120: **stands for**: will be accepted as; "stands" in the next line is a joking reference to an erection

121: **tarry**: delay, wait

121: Scene: **Ay, it stands . . . long**: In Lindsay Posner's 1999 RSC production when Sly (Stuart McQuarrie) said this, his "wife" (Ryan Pope) knocked him down and exited.

122: **loth**: unwilling

126: **meet**: appropriate

128: **nurse**: nourisher; **frenzy**: madness

131: **bars**: prevents

132: **Marry...comonty**: the First Folio reads "Marrie I will let them play, it is not a Comontie"; Capell (1768) first made this emendation with minor differences of spelling and punctuation. **comonty**: comedy

133: **gambold**: frolic, gambol; **tumbling trick**: acrobatic or balancing trick

134: **stuff**: goods, furnishings

139: **slip**: pass by

Or, if not so, until the sun be set.
For your physicians have expressly charged,
In peril to incur your former malady,
That I should yet absent me from your bed.
I hope this reason stands for my excuse.   120

SLY

Ay, it stands so that I may hardly tarry so long. But I would be
loth to fall into my dreams again. I will therefore tarry in despite
of the flesh and the blood.

Enter a MESSENGER

MESSENGER

Your honor's players, hearing your amendment,
Are come to play a pleasant comedy,   125
For so your doctors hold it very meet,
Seeing too much sadness hath congealed your blood,
And melancholy is the nurse of frenzy.
Therefore they thought it good you hear a play,
And frame your mind to mirth and merriment,   130
Which bars a thousand harms, and lengthens life.

SLY

Marry, I will. Let them play it. Is not a comonty a Christmas
gambold, or a tumbling trick?

PAGE

No, my good lord, it is more pleasing stuff.

SLY

What, household stuff?   135

PAGE

It is a kind of history.

SLY

Well, we'll see't.
Come, Madam wife, sit by my side,
And let the world slip; we shall ne'er be younger.

[The Taming of
the Shrew

Act 1

z.

0: Scene: no scene division here in the First Folio; Pope first made this division (1723-25)

0: Scene: In Lindsay Posner's 1999 RSC production, "Taming of the Shrew" came up on a screen at the back of the stage as if on a computer screen; the dialogue between Tranio (Louis Hilyer) and Lucentio (Jo Stone-Fewings, on horseback) was shown on film on that screen up to "learning and ingenious studies" (1.1.9) after which a door in the screen opened and Tranio and Lucentio entered the stage and continued the dialogue.

0: Stage Direction: *Flourish*: fanfare of trumpets

1: **for**: because of
2: **Padua, nursery of arts**: the University of Padua was famous as a centre of learning in Shakespeare's time
3: **arrived for**: arrived in or at
5: **leave**: permission
7: **approved**: found reliable, proved
8: **breathe**: pause, stay for a while; **haply institute**: perhaps begin
9: **ingenious**: intellectual, liberal
12: **great traffic**: substantial business, extensive trading
13: **Vincentio**: the First Folio reads "*Vincentio's*"; Thomas Hanmer first made this emendation (1744)
17: **for the time**: at present
19: **apply**: devote myself to
23: **plash**: pool, puddle
25: *Mi perdonato*: excuse me
26: **affected as**: feeling or inclined the same as
31: **stoics**: school of Greek philosophers who taught that men should be free from passions and equally indifferent to suffering and joy; **stocks**: unfeeling people, blocks of wood

Act 1, Scene 1]

Flourish. Enter LUCENTIO, and his man TRANIO

LUCENTIO

   Tranio, since for the great desire I had
   To see fair Padua, nursery of arts,
   I am arrived for fruitful Lombardy,
   The pleasant garden of great Italy,
   And by my father's love and leave am armed   5
   With his good will and thy good company.
   My trusty servant, well approved in all,
   Here let us breathe, and haply institute
   A course of learning and ingenious studies.
   Pisa renownèd for grave citizens   10
   Gave me my being, and my father first,
   A merchant of great traffic through the world,
   Vincentio, come of the Bentivolii.
   Vincentio's son, brought up in Florence,
   It shall become to serve all hopes conceived   15
   To deck his fortune with his virtuous deeds.
   And therefore, Tranio, for the time I study,
   Virtue and that part of philosophy
   Will I apply that treats of happiness,
   By virtue specially to be achieved.   20
   Tell me thy mind, for I have Pisa left
   And am to Padua come, as he that leaves
   A shallow plash to plunge him in the deep,
   And with satiety seeks to quench his thirst.

TRANIO

   Mi perdonato, gentle master mine.   25
   I am in all affected as yourself,
   Glad that you thus continue your resolve
   To suck the sweets of sweet philosophy.
   Only, good master, while we do admire
   This virtue and this moral discipline,   30
   Let's be no stoics, nor no stocks, I pray,

32: **devote**: devoted; **Aristotle's checks**: the restraint or restrictions advocated by Aristotle.

33: **As**: so that; **Ovid**: classical Roman poet; (his *Ars Amatoria* [*Art to Love*] is mentioned at 4.2.8); **abjured**: repudiated, renounced

34: **Balk logic**: chop logic

36: **quicken**: liven up

41: **Gramercies**: many thanks

42: **come ashore**: many commentators have taken this as indicating that Shakespeare thought that Pisa was a port, but Brian Morris (1981) points out that in Shakespeare's time it was well known that this part of Italy was a network of various kinds of waterways.

45: Stage Direction: **Enter BAPTISTA...BIÀNCA**: Appears with "*LUCENTIO and TRANIO stand by*" in the First Folio, but Lucentio's words ("what company is this?", 1.1.46) indicate that the entry occurs here. "*Suitor*" is "*sister*" in the First Folio; the Second Folio (1632) reads "*Shuiter*" and the Third Folio (1663) reads "*Suitor*"; **pantaloon**: foolish, ridiculous old man (a stock character in Renaissance Italian comedy)

50-51: "That is, not to bestow my youngest daughter / Before I have a husband for the elder": David Sabin as Baptista and Emery Battis as Gremio in the Shakespeare Theatre Company's 1994-1995 production directed by Adrian Hall
Photo: Carol Pratt

48-103: *Norman Tyrrell as Baptista, Sian Phillips as Katherina, Doria Noar as Bianca, and Ensemble*
Sean Baker as Baptista, Frances Barber as Katherina, Elizabeth Anne O'Brien as Bianca, and Ensemble

55: **cart**: As punishment, prostitutes were paraded around in an open cart.

58: **stale**: prostitute, also figure of fun; **mates**: contemptuous term meaning fellows or husbands

tracks 2-4

Or so devote to Aristotle's checks
As Ovid be an outcast quite abjured.
Balk logic with acquaintance that you have,
And practice rhetoric in your common talk.   35
Music and poesy use, to quicken you;
The mathematics and the metaphysics,
Fall to them as you find your stomach serves you.
No profit grows where is no pleasure ta'en:
In brief, sir, study what you most affect.   40

LUCENTIO
Gramercies, Tranio, well dost thou advise,
If, Biondello, thou wert come ashore,
We could at once put us in readiness,
And take a lodging fit to entertain
Such friends as time in Padua shall beget.   45
    Enter BAPTISTA with his two daughters,
            KATHERINA and BIANCA, GREMIO, a pantaloon,
            HORTENSIO[, suitor] to BIANCA
But stay a while, what company is this?

TRANIO
Master, some show to welcome us to town.
                                        LUCENTIO and TRANIO stand by

BAPTISTA
Gentlemen, importune me no farther,
For how I firmly am resolved you know:
That is, not to bestow my youngest daughter   50
Before I have a husband for the elder.
If either of you both love Katherina,
Because I know you well and love you well,
Leave shall you have to court her at your pleasure.

GREMIO
To cart her rather. She's too rough for me.   55
There, there, Hortensio, will you any wife?

KATHERINA
I pray you, sir, is it your will
To make a stale of me amongst these mates?

tracks 2-4

48-103: *Norman Tyrrell as Baptista, Sian Phillips as Katherina, Doria Noar as Bianca, and Ensemble*
Sean Baker as Baptista, Frances Barber as Katherina, Elizabeth Anne O'Brien as Bianca, and Ensemble

Costume rendering for Kate from the Oregon Shakespeare Festival's 2000
production directed by Kenneth Albers
Costume design: Susan E. Mickey. Courtesy of the Oregon Shakespeare Festival

59–60: Mates, maid...mold: appears as three lines in the First Folio with "No mates for you" as the second line

62: Iwis: certainly

64: noddle: head

65: paint your face: i.e., with blood from scratching

68: Husht: hush, be quiet; **toward**: about to take place

69: froward: willfully contrary, perverse

73: mum: keep quiet

78: peat: pet, darling; **put...why**: cry if she could find some excuse

HORTENSIO
  Mates, maid, how mean you that? No mates for you,
  Unless you were of gentler milder mold.   60

KATHERINA
  I' faith sir, you shall never need to fear;
  Iwis it is not halfway to her heart.
  But if it were, doubt not her care should be
  To comb your noddle with a three-legged stool,
  And paint your face, and use you like a fool.   65

HORTENSIO
  From all such devils, good Lord deliver us.

GREMIO
  And me too, good Lord.

TRANIO
  Husht, master, here's some good pastime toward;
  That wench is stark mad, or wonderful froward.

LUCENTIO
  But in the other's silence do I see,   70
  Maid's mild behavior and sobriety.
  Peace, Tranio.

TRANIO
  Well said, master; mum, and gaze your fill.

BAPTISTA
  Gentlemen, that I may soon make good
  What I have said — Bianca, get you in,   75
  And let it not displease thee, good Bianca,
  For I will love thee ne'er the less, my girl.

KATHERINA
  A pretty peat! It is best put finger in the eye, and she knew why.

tracks 2-4

48-103: *Norman Tyrrell as Baptista, Sian Phillips as Katherina, Doria Noar as Bianca, and Ensemble*
Sean Baker as Baptista, Frances Barber as Katherina, Elizabeth Anne O'Brien as Bianca, and Ensemble

80: **subscribe**: submit

80-82: Scene: **Sir...myself**: In Franco Zeffirelli's 1966 film Bianca (Natasha Pyne) catches sight of Lucentio (Michael York) nearby, so she says these lines to her father with exaggerated sweetness and submission for Lucentio's benefit.

83: **Minerva**: goddess of wisdom and patroness of the arts
84: **strange**: reserved, distant, unfriendly
86: **mew her up**: shut her up, put her in a cage
88: **her...her**: The first "her" is Bianca and the second is Katherina.
96: **Prefer**: recommend; **cunning**: talented, learned
100: **commune with**: tell, communicate to

101: Scene: **I trust...not?**: Fiona Shaw has said of Miller's 1987 RSC production that at this point, Baptista (George Raistrick) "hesitated as if he'd forgotten her name before saying 'Katherina, you may stay,'...Kate has to demand her right to go into the house" In Doran's 2003 RSC production, Katherina (Alexandra Gilbreath) ran to the house, but the door slammed in her face; she bellowed, banged on it, and kicked it until it opened. In Taichman's 2007 Shakespeare Theatre Company Production in Washington, DC, Katherina (Charlayne Woodard) tried to go in but the revolving door would not turn.

Mary Pickford as Katherina in the 1929 film directed by Sam Taylor
Courtesy of Douglas Lanier

102: **belike**: as seems likely or probable

BIANCA
    Sister, content you in my discontent.
    Sir, to your pleasure humbly I subscribe.   80
    My books and instruments shall be my company,
    On them to look and practice by myself.

LUCENTIO
    Hark, Tranio, thou mayst hear Minerva speak.

HORTENSIO
    Signor Baptista, will you be so strange?
    Sorry am I that our good will effects   85
    Bianca's grief.

GREMIO
             Why will you mew her up,
    Signor Baptista, for this fiend of hell,
    And make her bear the penance of her tongue?

BAPTISTA
    Gentlemen, content ye. I am resolved.
    Go in, Bianca.   90
                 [Exit BIANCA]

    And for I know she taketh most delight
    In music, instruments, and poetry,
    Schoolmasters will I keep within my house
    Fit to instruct her youth. If you, Hortensio,
    Or, Signor Gremio, you know any such,   95
    Prefer them hither; for to cunning men
    I will be very kind, and liberal
    To mine own children in good bringing up.
    And so farewell. Katherina, you may stay,
    For I have more to commune with Bianca.   100
                 Exit

KATHERINA
    Why, and I trust I may go too, may I not?
    What, shall I be appointed hours, as though, belike,
    I knew not what to take and what to leave? Ha!

                 Exit

104: **devil's dam**: devil's mother (The devil's mother was believed to be worse than the devil.)

105: **Their love**: perhaps the love of women. Some editors (e.g., G. R. Hibbard, 1968) argue that this should read "There! Love"

106: **blow...together**: wait patiently

106–107: **Our cake's...sides**: we have both failed (proverbial)

109: **wish**: commend

111: **brooked parle**: allowed negotiations; **advice**: consideration

112: **toucheth**: concerns

120: **very a fool**: completely a fool

122: **alarums**: disturbances, scoldings

123: **and**: if; **light on**: happen upon, find

125: **had as lief**: would as willingly, would as soon

126: **at the high cross**: at the center of the town (where a cross would be on a pedestal)

GREMIO

You may go to the devil's dam. Your gifts are so good here's none
will hold you. Their love is not so great, Hortensio, but we may   105
blow our nails together, and fast it fairly out. Our cake's dough on
both sides. Farewell. Yet, for the love I bear my sweet Bianca, if I
can by any means light on a fit man to teach her that wherein she
delights, I will wish him to her father.

HORTENSIO

So will I, Signor Gremio. But a word, I pray. Though the nature   110
of our quarrel yet never brooked parle, know now upon advice, it
toucheth us both, that we may yet again have access to our fair
mistress, and be happy rivals in Bianca's love, to labor and effect
one thing specially.

GREMIO

What's that, I pray?   115

HORTENSIO

Marry, sir, to get a husband for her sister.

GREMIO

A husband? A devil.

HORTENSIO

I say a husband.

GREMIO

I say a devil. Think'st thou, Hortensio, though her father be very
rich, any man is so very a fool to be married to hell?   120

HORTENSIO

Tush, Gremio, though it pass your patience and mine to endure
her loud alarums, why man there be good fellows in the world,
and a man could light on them, would take her with all faults, and
money enough.

GREMIO

I cannot tell, but I had as lief take her dowry with this condition: 125
to be whipped at the high cross every morning.

128: **bar in law**: legal impediment

130–131: **have to't afresh**: start the rivalry up again

131: **Happy...dole**: a proverbial expression roughly equivalent to "May the best man win."

133: **would I**: I wish that I had

135: Stage Direction: ***Exeunt [GREMIO and HORTENSIO]***: The First Folio reads "*Exeunt ambo*"; Rowe made this emendation first (1709). ***Manet***: remains

141: **I found...idleness**: i.e., I fell in love. (The juice of the flower known as "love in idleness," heartsease, was believed to bring about love, as in *A Midsummer Night's Dream* where Puck uses it in this way [2.1.168]. There is also a reference to the proverbial notion that idleness breeds love.)

143: **secret**: trusted

144: **Anna...Carthage**: In Virgil's *Aeneid*, Anna, sister of Dido Queen of Carthage, is the queen's confidante and knows the secret of Dido's love for Aeneas. (See also Christopher Marlowe's 1594 play *Dido, Queen of Carthage*)

150: **Affection...heart**: i.e., it is not possible to make love go away by scolding

152: ***Redime...minimo***: ransom yourself from captivity at the lowest possible cost; ***captum***: The First Folio reads "*captam*"; the Second Folio (1632) reads "*captum*".

HORTENSIO
    Faith, as you say, there's small choice in rotten apples. But come,
    since this bar in law makes us friends, it shall be so far forth
    friendly maintained, till by helping Baptista's eldest daughter to
    a husband, we set his youngest free for a husband, and then have   130
    to't afresh. Sweet Bianca! Happy man be his dole. He that runs
    fastest gets the ring. How say you, Signor Gremio?

GREMIO
    I am agreed, and would I had given him the best horse in Padua
    to begin his wooing that would thoroughly woo her, wed her, and
    bed her, and rid the house of her. Come on.   135
                    Exeunt [GREMIO and HORTENSIO]
                    Manet TRANIO and LUCENTIO

TRANIO
    I pray sir tell me, is it possible
    That love should of a sudden take such hold?

LUCENTIO
    Oh Tranio, till I found it to be true,
    I never thought it possible or likely.
    But see, while idly I stood looking on,   140
    I found the effect of love in idleness,
    And now in plainness do confess to thee
    That art to me as secret and as dear
    As Anna to the Queen of Carthage was,
    Tranio I burn, I pine, I perish, Tranio,   145
    If I achieve not this young modest girl.
    Counsel me, Tranio, for I know thou canst;
    Assist me, Tranio, for I know thou wilt.

TRANIO
    Master, it is no time to chide you now;
    Affection is not rated from the heart.   150
    If love have touched you, naught remains but so,
    Redime te captum quam queas minimo.

156: **pith of all**: central issue, most important point

158: **daughter of Agenor**: i.e., Europa. Europa's beauty caused Jove (Jupiter) to appear to her in the form of a white bull; he then carried her off on his back to Crete.

160: **strand**: shore

170: **curst**: quarrelsome, bad-tempered; **shrewd**: shrewish, sharp-tongued

174: **Because**: so that

LUCENTIO

Gramercies, lad. Go forward. This contents;
The rest will comfort, for thy counsel's sound.

TRANIO

Master, you looked so longly on the maid,   155
Perhaps you marked not what's the pith of all.

LUCENTIO

Oh yes, I saw sweet beauty in her face,
Such as the daughter of Agenor had,
That made great Jove to humble him to her hand,
When with his knees he kissed the Cretan strand.   160

TRANIO

Saw you no more? Marked you not how her sister
Began to scold and raise up such a storm
That mortal ears might hardly endure the din?

LUCENTIO

Tranio, I saw her coral lips to move,
And with her breath she did perfume the air.   165
Sacred and sweet was all I saw in her.

TRANIO

Nay, then, 'tis time to stir him from his trance.
I pray, awake, sir. If you love the maid,
Bend thoughts and wits to achieve her. Thus it stands:
Her elder sister is so curst and shrewd   170
That till the father rid his hands of her,
Master, your love must live a maid at home,
And therefore has he closely mewed her up,
Because she will not be annoyed with suitors.

LUCENTIO

Ah, Tranio, what a cruel father's he.   175
But art thou not advised, he took some care
To get her cunning schoolmasters to instruct her?

179: **for my hand**: by my hand
180: **meet...one**: agree and work together
183: **device**: plan, scheme
186: **Keep...his book**: entertain guests and study
188: *Basta*: enough; **I have it full**: I have worked it all out
193: **port**: style of living
195: **meaner**: poorer, of lower social standing
197: **Uncase thee**: take off your clothes; **take...cloak**: Servants wore blue clothing, so by wearing Lucentio's clothing, Tranio will be dressed like a gentleman.

197: "Uncase thee; take my colored hat and cloak": Mark Rylance as Lucentio and John Bowe as Tranio in the Royal Shakespeare Company's 1982 production directed by Barry Kyle
Photo: Donald Cooper

199: **charm...tongue**: influence or force him to keep quiet

TRANIO
  Ay, marry am I, sir, and now 'tis plotted.

LUCENTIO
  I have it, Tranio.

TRANIO
                 Master, for my hand,
  Both our inventions meet and jump in one.   180

LUCENTIO
  Tell me thine first.

TRANIO
                 You will be schoolmaster
  And undertake the teaching of the maid;
  That's your device.

LUCENTIO
                It is. May it be done?

TRANIO
  Not possible; for who shall bear your part
  And be in Padua here Vincentio's son,   185
  Keep house, and ply his book, welcome his friends,
  Visit his countrymen and banquet them?

LUCENTIO
  Basta, content thee, for I have it full.
  We have not yet been seen in any house,
  Nor can we be distinguished by our faces   190
  For man or master. Then it follows thus:
  Thou shalt be master, Tranio, in my stead,
  Keep house, and port, and servants, as I should.
  I will some other be, some Florentine,
  Some Neapolitan, or meaner man of Pisa.   195
  'Tis hatched, and shall be so. Tranio, at once
  Uncase thee; take my colored hat and cloak.
  When Biondello comes, he waits on thee,
  But I will charm him first to keep his tongue.

201: **sith**: since

202: **tied**: obliged

204: **quoth**: said

210: **thralled**: enthralled, captivated

216: **frame**: adapt, adjust

218: **countenance**: manner, outward appearance

221: **descried**: recognized, observed

224: **ne'er a whit**: not at all

TRANIO
    So had you need.   200
    In brief, sir, sith it your pleasure is,
    And I am tied to be obedient—
    For so your father charged me at our parting:
    "Be serviceable to my son," quoth he
    Although I think 'twas in another sense—   205
    I am content to be Lucentio,
    Because so well I love Lucentio.

LUCENTIO
    Tranio, be so, because Lucentio loves,
    And let me be a slave, t'achieve that maid
    Whose sudden sight hath thralled my wounded eye.   210
                                    Enter BIONDELLO
    Here comes the rogue. Sirrah, where have you been?

BIONDELLO
    Where have I been? Nay, how now, where are you? Master, has
    my fellow Tranio stolen your clothes, or you stolen his, or both?
    Pray, what's the news?

LUCENTIO
    Sirrah, come hither. 'Tis no time to jest,   215
    And therefore frame your manners to the time.
    Your fellow Tranio here, to save my life,
    Puts my apparel and my countenance on,
    And I for my escape have put on his.
    For in a quarrel since I came ashore,   220
    I killed a man, and fear I was descried.
    Wait you on him, I charge you, as becomes,
    While I make way from hence to save my life.
    You understand me?

BIONDELLO
                        Aye sir, ne'er a whit.

LUCENTIO
    And not a jot of Tranio in your mouth;   225
    Tranio is changed into Lucentio.

Michael Medico as Lucentio dressed as Cambio in the Shakespeare
Theatre Company's 1994-1995 production directed by Adrian Hall
Photo: Carol Pratt

228–233: **So could…Lucentio**: prose in the First Folio; Capell (1768) first set as verse

233: **your**: The First Folio reads "you"; the Second Folio (1632) reads "your".

235: **rests**: remains to be done

237SD-243: ***The Presenters…'twere done***: from the quarto of 1594

237: Stage Direction: ***[speak]***: the First Folio reads *"speaks"*; Brian Morris made this emendation (1981)

238: Speech Prefix: **LORD**: the First Folio reads "1. *Man*."; G. R. Hibbard (1968) first made this emendation

238: **mind**: pay attention to

BIONDELLO
  The better for him; would I were so, too.

TRANIO
  So could I, faith, boy, to have the next wish after,
  That Lucentio indeed had Baptista's youngest daughter.
  But, sirrah, not for my sake, but your master's, I advise   230
  You use your manners discreetly in all kind of companies.
  When I am alone, why then I am Tranio,
  But in all places else, your master Lucentio.

LUCENTIO
  Tranio, let's go.
  One thing more rests, that thy self execute: 235
  To make one among these wooers. If thou ask me why,
  Sufficeth my reasons are both good and weighty.

                                                                  Exeunt
                                              The Presenters above [speak]

LORD
  My Lord, you nod; you do not mind the play.

SLY
  Yes, by Saint Anne, do I. A good matter surely.
  Comes there any more of it?   240

LADY
  My lord, 'tis but begun.

SLY
  'Tis a very excellent piece of work, madam lady; would 'twere
  done.
                                              They sit and mark

0: Scene: There is no scene division in the First Folio; Capell (1768) first made this division.

4: **trow**: believe

6-7: "Knock, sir? Whom should I knock? Is there any man has rebused / your worship?": Jay O. Sanders as Petruchio and Mario Cantone as Grumio in the 1999 Joseph Papp Public Theater production directed by Mel Shapiro
Photo: Michal Daniel

6: **rebused**: Grumio's mistaken version of "abused"
8: **knock me**: knock on the door for me; Grumio interprets this as an instruction to hit Petruchio.
12: **pate**: head
13–14: **I should...the worst**: appears as three lines in the First Folio ("I should knock you first" is second line); Theobald (1733) first made this division. Grumio means that if he were to hit Petruchio, Petruchio would have an excuse to hit him, and Grumio would come off worse.
16: **ring**: a pun on "wring"
17: **sol, fa**: sing a scale

Act 1, Scene 2]

Enter PETRUCHIO, and his man GRUMIO

PETRUCHIO
    Verona, for a while I take my leave,
    To see my friends in Padua, but of all
    My best belovèd and approvèd friend
    Hortensio; and I trow this is his house.
    Here, sirrah Grumio, knock, I say.   5

GRUMIO
    Knock, sir? Whom should I knock? Is there any man has rebused
    your worship?

PETRUCHIO
    Villain, I say, knock me here soundly.

GRUMIO
    Knock you here, sir? Why, sir, what am I, sir, that I should knock
    you here, sir?   10

PETRUCHIO
    Villain, I say, knock me at this gate,
    And rap me well, or I'll knock your knave's pate.

GRUMIO
    My master is grown quarrelsome. I should knock you first,
    And then I know after who comes by the worst.

PETRUCHIO
    Will it not be?   15
    'Faith sirrah, and you'll not knock, I'll ring it,
    I'll try how you can *sol, fa* and sing it.

                  He wrings him by the ears

GRUMIO
    Help, mistress, help! My master is mad.

Costume rendering for Petruchio from the Oregon Shakespeare Festival's 2000
production directed by Kenneth Albers
Costume design: Susan E. Mickey. Courtesy of the Oregon Shakespeare Festival

22: **part the fray**: stop the fight

23: ***Con tutto il core ben trovato***: The First Folio reads *Contutti le core bene trobatto*.
Editors, e.g., Rowe (1709) and Theobald (1733), have corrected Shakespeare's irregular
Italian. The phrase means, "With all my heart I am glad to see you."

24–25: ***Alla nostra...mio Petruchio***: The First Folio reads *Alla nostra casa bene venuto
multo honorata signior mio Petruchio,* set as prose. The Second Folio (1632) corrects
the Italian but leaves it as prose. The lines mean, "Welcome to our house, my much-
honored Master Petruchio."

26: **compound**: settle

27: **'leges**: alleges; **in Latin**: Grumio, supposedly Italian, mistakes Italian for Latin

30–31: **two...out**: (referring to Petruchio) somewhat crazy or possibly drunk (the
phrase is an allusion to the card game "one and thirty", in which to have a score of
32 meant overshooting by 1 and getting it wrong)

PETRUCHIO
Now knock when I bid you, sirrah villain.

Enter HORTENSIO

HORTENSIO
How now, what's the matter? My old friend Grumio, and my good   20
friend Petruchio? How do you all at Verona?

PETRUCHIO
Signor Hortensio, come you to part the fray?
Con tutto il core ben trovato, may I say.

HORTENSIO
Alla nostra casa ben venuto
Molto honorato signor mio Petruchio.   25
Rise, Grumio, rise. We will compound this quarrel.

GRUMIO
Nay 'tis no matter sir, what he 'leges in Latin. If this be not a law-
ful cause for me to leave his service, look you, sir. He bid me
knock him, and rap him soundly, sir. Well, was it fit for a servant
to use his master so, being perhaps, for ought I see, two and thirty,   30
a pip out?

Whom would to God I had well knocked at first,
Then had not Grumio come by the worst.

PETRUCHIO
A senseless villain, good Hortensio.
I bade the rascal knock upon your gate   35
And could not get him for my heart to do it.

GRUMIO
Knock at the gate? Oh heavens, spake you not these words plain:
"Sirrah, knock me here, rap me here, knock me well, and knock
me soundly"? And come you now with knocking at the gate?

PETRUCHIO
Sirrah, be gone, or talk not I advise you.   40

41: **I am Grumio's pledge**: i.e., I am the guarantor of Grumio's good behavior

42: **this'**: this is

43: **ancient**: long-standing

48: **experience grows. But in a few**: The First Folio reads "experience growes but in a few"; Hanmer (1744) emended the text to "experience grows; but in a few". "Few" here means "few words".

51: **maze**: uncertain, unpredictable course

52: **Happily**: with luck

53: **Crowns**: gold coins

55: **come roundly**: speak plainly

56: **ill-favored**: ugly or unattractive; "ill-favored" must refer to Katherina's unpleasant nature rather than her physical appearance as Hortensio later calls her "beauteous"(1.2.81).

64: **burden**: purpose, basis; also refers to musical accompaniment

65: **Be she...love**: In Gower's *Confessio Amantis*, Florentius marries an ugly old woman to save his life; Chaucer's Wife of Bath tells the same story.

66: **Sibyl**: In classical legends there were several Sibyls who were prophetesses.

67: **Socrates' Xanthippe**: i.e., Socrates' wife (whose bad temper made her proverbial for a shrewish wife)

68: **moves**: bothers, troubles

69: **were she as**: The First Folio reads "she is as"; this emendation appears in the 1631 quarto.

HORTENSIO

    Petruchio, patience. I am Grumio's pledge.
    Why, this' a heavy chance twixt him and you,
    Your ancient, trusty, pleasant servant Grumio.
    And tell me now, sweet friend, what happy gale
    Blows you to Padua here from old Verona?   45

PETRUCHIO

    Such wind as scatters young men through the world
    To seek their fortunes farther than at home,
    Where small experience grows. But in a few,
    Signor Hortensio, thus it stands with me:
    Antonio, my father, is deceased,   50
    And I have thrust myself into this maze,
    Happily to wive and thrive, as best I may.
    Crowns in my purse I have, and goods at home,
    And so am come abroad to see the world.

HORTENSIO

    Petruchio, shall I then come roundly to thee   55
    And wish thee to a shrewd ill-favored wife?
    Thou'dst thank me but a little for my counsel,
    And yet I'll promise thee she shall be rich,
    And very rich. But th'art too much my friend,
    And I'll not wish thee to her.   60

PETRUCHIO

    Signor Hortensio, 'twixt such friends as we
    Few words suffice; and therefore, if thou know
    One rich enough to be Petruchio's wife
    (As wealth is burden of my wooing dance),
    Be she as foul as was Florentius' love,   65
    As old as Sibyl, and as curst and shrewd
    As Socrates' Xanthippe, or a worse,
    She moves me not, or not removes at least
    Affection's edge in me, were she as rough
    As are the swelling Adriatic seas.   70
    I come to wive it wealthily in Padua;
    If wealthily, then happily in Padua.

74: **aglet baby**: small figure-shaped tag on the end of a lace or possibly a doll decorated with spangles or other metallic decorations

75: **trot**: hag

77: **so**: if; **withal**: with it

78: **stepped thus far in**: gone so far

88-89: "Thou know'st not gold's effect. / Tell me her father's name and 'tis enough": Jonathan Epstein as Petruchio, Robert Carin as Hortensio and Floyd King as Grumio in the Shakespeare Theatre Company's 1994-1995 production directed by Adrian Hall
Photo: Carol Pratt

90: **board**: woo

100: **give you over**: leave you

GRUMIO

    Nay look you, sir, he tells you flatly what his mind is. Why, give
    him gold enough, and marry him to a puppet or an aglet baby, or
    an old trot with ne'er a tooth in her head, though she have as   75
    many diseases as two and fifty horses. Why, nothing comes amiss,
    so money comes withal.

HORTENSIO

    Petruchio, since we are stepped thus far in,
    I will continue that I broached in jest.
    I can, Petruchio, help thee to a wife   80
    With wealth enough, and young and beauteous,
    Brought up as best becomes a gentlewoman.
    Her only fault, and that is faults enough,
    Is, that she is intolerable curst,
    And shrewd, and froward, so beyond all measure   85
    That, were my state far worser than it is,
    I would not wed her for a mine of gold.

PETRUCHIO

    Hortensio, peace. Thou know'st not gold's effect.
    Tell me her father's name, and 'tis enough;
    For I will board her, though she chide as loud   90
    As thunder when the clouds in Autumn crack.

HORTENSIO

    Her father is Baptista Minola,
    An affable and courteous gentleman;
    Her name is Katherina Minola,
    Renowned in Padua for her scolding tongue.   95

PETRUCHIO

    I know her father, though I know not her,
    And he knew my deceaséd father well.
    I will not sleep, Hortensio, till I see her,
    And therefore let me be thus bold with you
    To give you over at this first encounter,   100
    Unless you will accompany me thither.

102: **A' my word, and**: on my word, if

104: **half a score**: i.e., ten

105–106: **and he...tricks**: This passage is obscure, and editors have offered many differing explanations. It may mean that Petruchio will insult and scold her more strongly than she can him, with a possible misused reference to rhetoric.

106: **stand**: stand up to, resist

107: **figure**: i.e., figure of speech

110: **Tarry**: wait

111: **keep**: keeping, custody

112: **hold**: safekeeping

114: **me and other**: The First Folio reads "me. Other"; Hanmer (1744) made the emendation to "me, and other"; **other more**: others as well

117: **rehearsed**: enumerated, listed

124: **do me grace**: do me a favor

127: **Well seen**: well qualified

GRUMIO

I pray you, Sir, let him go while the humor lasts. A' my word, and
she knew him as well as I do, she would think scolding would do
little good upon him. She may perhaps call him half a score
knaves or so. Why, that's nothing; and he begin once, he'll rail in   105
his rope tricks. I'll tell you what, sir, and she stand him but a
little, he will throw a figure in her face, and so disfigure her with
it, that she shall have no more eyes to see withal than a cat. You
know him not, sir.

HORTENSIO

Tarry, Petruchio, I must go with thee,   110
For in Baptista's keep my treasure is.
He hath the jewel of my life in hold,
His youngest daughter, beautiful Bianca,
And her withholds from me and other more,
Suitors to her and rivals in my love,   115
Supposing it a thing impossible,
For those defects I have before rehearsed,
That ever Katherina will be wooed.
Therefore this order hath Baptista ta'en,
That none shall have access unto Bianca   120
Till Katherine the curst have got a husband.

GRUMIO

"Katherine the curst,"
A title for a maid of all titles the worst.

HORTENSIO

Now shall my friend Petruchio do me grace,
And offer me disguised in sober robes   125
To old Baptista as a schoolmaster
Well seen in music, to instruct Bianca,
That so I may by this device at least
Have leave and leisure to make love to her,
And unsuspected court her by herself.   130
                    Enter GREMIO and LUCENTIO disguised

135: Stage Direction: *[They stand aside]*: not in the First Folio; Capell (1768) has *"they retire"* at line 147

136: **proper stripling**: handsome youth (sarcastic description of Gremio)

137: **note**: i.e., Lucentio's list of books

139: **see...hand**: see to that in any case

143: **mend it with a largess**: improve it with a substantial gift

144: **them**: i.e., the books

149: **As firmly as...place**: as if you yourself were present all the time

153: **woodcock**: dupe, simpleton (The woodcock was an easy bird to catch and thus became proverbial for stupidity.)

GRUMIO
    Here's no knavery. See, to beguile the old folks, how the young
    folks lay their heads together. Master, master, look about you.
    Who goes there, ha?

HORTENSIO
    Peace, Grumio, it is the rival of my love.
    Petruchio, stand by a while.   135
                                                    [They stand aside]

GRUMIO
    A proper stripling, and an amorous.

GREMIO
    Oh, very well, I have perused the note.
    Hark you, sir, I'll have them very fairly bound,
    All books of love, see that at any hand,
    And see you read no other lectures to her.   140
    You understand me. Over and beside
    Signor Baptista's liberality,
    I'll mend it with a largess. Take your paper too,
    And let me have them very well perfumed,
    For she is sweeter than perfume itself   145
    To whom they go to. What will you read to her?

LUCENTIO
    Whate'er I read to her, I'll plead for you,
    As for my patron, stand you so assured,
    As firmly as yourself were still in place,
    Yea, and perhaps with more successful words   150
    Than you, unless you were a scholar, sir.

GREMIO
    Oh, this learning, what a thing it is!

GRUMIO
    Oh, this woodcock, what an ass it is!

PETRUCHIO
    Peace, sirrah.

155: Stage Direction: *[Coming forward]*: not in the First Folio; Capell (1768) has *"advancing"*.

157: **Trow**: know

162: **Fit for her turn**: right for her needs

165: **help me**: The First Folio reads "helpe one"; Rowe (1709) made this emendation.

170: Stage Direction: *[Aside]*: not in the First Folio; Capell (1768) first made this emendation

170: **bags**: wealth (moneybags)

171: **vent**: express

173: **indifferent**: equally

175: **Upon...liking**: if we come to terms that suit him

178: **So said...well**: it is good if deeds match words

HORTENSIO
Grumio, mum. [*Coming forward*] God save you, Signor Gremio.   155

GREMIO
And you are well met, Signor Hortensio.
Trow you whither I am going? To Baptista Minola.
I promised to enquire carefully
About a schoolmaster for the fair Bianca,
And by good fortune I have lighted well   160
On this young man, for learning and behavior
Fit for her turn, well read in poetry
And other books, good ones, I warrant ye.

HORTENSIO
'Tis well. And I have met a gentleman
Hath promised me to help me to another,   165
A fine musician to instruct our mistress.
So shall I no whit be behind in duty
To fair Bianca, so beloved of me.

GREMIO
Beloved of me, and that my deeds shall prove.

GRUMIO
[*Aside*] And that his bags shall prove.   170

HORTENSIO
Gremio, 'tis now no time to vent our love.
Listen to me, and if you speak me fair,
I'll tell you news indifferent good for either.
Here is a gentleman whom by chance I met,
Upon agreement from us to his liking,   175
Will undertake to woo curst Katherine,
Yea, and to marry her, if her dowry please.

GREMIO
So said, so done, is well.
Hortensio, have you told him all her faults?

183: **Antonio's**: The First Folio reads "Butonios"; Rowe (1709) first made this emendation.

186: **were strange**: would be unlikely

187: **stomach**: appetite, inclination, liking; **to't a**: get on with it in

189: **Will I live?**: yes, certainly (an idiomatic expression used to reply affirmatively)

196: **ordnance**: mounted guns, cannon

199: **'larums**: alarums, calls to arms

203: **fear...bugs**: frighten boys with imaginary beings or hobgoblins

PETRUCHIO

I know she is an irksome, brawling scold.   180
If that be all, masters, I hear no harm.

GREMIO

No, say'st me so, friend? What countryman?

PETRUCHIO

Born in Verona, old Antonio's son.
My father dead, my fortune lives for me,
And I do hope good days and long to see.   185

GREMIO

Oh sir, such a life with such a wife were strange.
But if you have a stomach, to't a God's name,
You shall have me assisting you in all.
But will you woo this wildcat?

PETRUCHIO

                Will I live?

GRUMIO

Will he woo her? Ay, or I'll hang her.   190

PETRUCHIO

Why came I hither but to that intent?
Think you a little din can daunt mine ears?
Have I not in my time heard lions roar?
Have I not heard the sea, puffed up with winds,
Rage like an angry boar chafèd with sweat?   195
Have I not heard great ordnance in the field,
And heaven's artillery thunder in the skies?
Have I not in a pitchèd battle heard
Loud 'larums, neighing steeds, and trumpets' clang?
And do you tell me of a woman's tongue,   200
That gives not half so great a blow to hear
As will a chestnut in a farmer's fire?
Tush, tush, fear boys with bugs.

208: **charge**: expense

210: Stage Direction: ***brave***: finely dressed

212: **readiest**: most convenient, shortest

217: **what have you to do?**: what business is it of yours?

218: **at any hand**: in any case

GRUMIO

For he fears none.

GREMIO

Hortensio, hark.
This Gentleman is happily arrived,   205
My mind presumes, for his own good, and yours.

HORTENSIO

I promised we would be contributors
And bear his charge of wooing, whatsoe'er.

GREMIO.

And so we will, provided that he win her.

GRUMIO

I would I were as sure of a good dinner.   210

Enter TRANIO brave, and BIONDELLO

TRANIO

Gentlemen, God save you. If I may be bold,
Tell me, I beseech you, which is the readiest way
To the house of Signor Baptista Minola?

BIONDELLO

He that has the two fair daughters—is't he you mean?

TRANIO

Even he, Biondello.   215

GREMIO

Hark you, sir, you mean not her to—

TRANIO

Perhaps him and her, sir; what have you to do?

PETRUCHIO

Not her that chides, sir, at any hand, I pray.

224: streets: The First Folio reads "streers"; this correction appears in the 1631 quarto.

228: choice: chosen

CJ Wilson as Tranio and Robert Carin as Hortensio in the Shakespeare Theatre Company's 1994-1995 production directed by Adrian Hall
Photo: Carol Pratt

TRANIO
I love no chiders, sir. Biondello, let's away.

LUCENTIO
Well begun, Tranio.

HORTENSIO
                Sir, a word ere you go.   220
Are you a suitor to the maid you talk of, yea or no?

TRANIO
And if I be sir, is it any offense?

GREMIO
No, if without more words you will get you hence.

TRANIO
Why, sir, I pray are not the streets as free
For me as for you?

GREMIO
                But so is not she.   225

TRANIO
For what reason, I beseech you?

GREMIO
For this reason if you'll know,
That she's the choice love of Signor Gremio.

HORTENSIO
That she's the chosen of Signor Hortensio.

TRANIO
Softly, my masters. If you be gentlemen,   230
Do me this right: hear me with patience.
Baptista is a noble gentleman,
To whom my father is not all unknown,
And were his daughter fairer than she is,

236: **Leda's daughter**: i.e., Helen of Troy

239: **Though Paris...alone**: though Paris (who stole Helen of Troy away from her husband) came hoping to be the only successful one

241: **give him...jade**: let him say or do what he wishes; he'll soon be tired and give up (a jade is a worn-out or worthless horse).

248: **let her go by**: leave her alone

249–50: **great Hercules...Alcides' twelve**: Petruchio is taking on a task perhaps more demanding than the twelve labors performed by Hercules (also known as Alcides) in Greek and Roman mythology

251: **sooth**: truth

252: **hearken for**: yearn for, want to win

She may more suitors have, and me for one.   235
Fair Leda's daughter had a thousand wooers,
Then well one more may fair Bianca have;
And so she shall. Lucentio shall make one,
Though Paris came in hope to speed alone.

GREMIO
What, this gentleman will out-talk us all.   240

LUCENTIO
Sir, give him head; I know he'll prove a jade.

PETRUCHIO
Hortensio, to what end are all these words?

HORTENSIO
Sir, let me be so bold as ask you,
Did you yet ever see Baptista's daughter?

TRANIO
No, sir, but hear I do that he hath two: 245
The one, as famous for a scolding tongue,
As is the other for beauteous modesty.

PETRUCHIO
Sir, sir, the first's for me; let her go by.

GREMIO
Yea, leave that labor to great Hercules,
And let it be more than Alcides' twelve.   250

PETRUCHIO
Sir, understand you this of me in sooth:
The youngest daughter whom you hearken for,
Her father keeps from all access of suitors,
And will not promise her to any man,
Until the elder sister first be wed.   255
The younger then is free, and not before.

258: **stead**: help

259: **feat**: The First Folio reads "seeke"; Rowe (1709) made this emendation.

261: **whose hap**: whose luck or good fortune

262: **Will...ingrate**: will not be so ill-mannered as to be ungrateful

263: **conceive**: understand

265: **gratify**: reward

266: **rest generally beholding**: are all indebted

268: **contrive**: while away

269: **quaff carouses**: drink toasts

272: **motion**: suggestion, proposal

274: ***ben venuto***: The First Folio reads "*Been venuto*"; the Second Folio (1632) corrects to "*ben*". The words literally mean "welcome", but here, Hortensio is offering to pay for Petruchio.

TRANIO
   If it be so, sir, that you are the man
   Must stead us all, and me amongst the rest,
   And if you break the ice, and do this feat,
   Achieve the elder, set the younger free   260
   For our access, whose hap shall be to have her
   Will not so graceless be to be ingrate.

HORTENSIO
   Sir, you say well, and well you do conceive,
   And since you do profess to be a suitor,
   You must, as we do, gratify this gentleman,   265
   To whom we all rest generally beholding.

TRANIO
   Sir, I shall not be slack, in sign whereof,
   Please ye we may contrive this afternoon,
   And quaff carouses to our mistress' health,
   And do as adversaries do in law,   270
   Strive mightily, but eat and drink as friends.

GRUMIO and BIONDELLO
   Oh excellent motion! Fellows, let's be gone.

HORTENSIO
   The motion's good indeed, and be it so,
   Petruchio, I shall be your *ben venuto*.

                                              Exeunt

The Taming of
the Shrew

Act 2
2.

o: **Scene**: no act or scene division at this point in the First Folio; Pope first made the division (1723-5). (The First Folio does not mark Act 2 at all; the next act or scene division is *"Actus Tertia"* at the beginning of Act 3.)

8-36:
Norman Tyrrell as Baptista, Sian Phillips as Katherina, and Doria Noar as Bianca

2: **bondmaid**: slave; in this case literally bound
3: **goods**: finery, clothing

8-9: "Of all thy suitors here I charge thee tell / Whom thou lov'st best": Tracey Ullman as Katherina and Helen Hunt as Bianca in the 1989-90 Public Theatre production directed by A. J. Antoon
Photo: George E. Joseph

8: **charge thee tell**: The First Folio reads "charge tell"; this emendation appears in the Second Folio (1632).
12: **fancy**: love
13: **Minion**: minx, spoilt brat
17: **fair**: finely dressed
18: **envy**: hate

Act 2, Scene 1]

BIANCA
Good sister, wrong me not, nor wrong yourself,
To make a bondmaid and a slave of me.
That I disdain. But for these other goods,
Unbind my hands, I'll pull them off myself,
Yea all my raiment, to my petticoat,   5
Or what you will command me, will I do,
So well I know my duty to my elders.

KATHERINA
Of all thy suitors here I charge thee tell
Whom thou lov'st best. See thou dissemble not.

BIANCA
Believe me, sister, of all the men alive   10
I never yet beheld that special face
Which I could fancy, more than any other.

KATHERINA
Minion, thou liest. Is't not Hortensio?

BIANCA
If you affect him, sister, here I swear
I'll plead for you myself, but you shall have him.   15

KATHERINA
Oh, then belike you fancy riches more;
You will have Gremio to keep you fair.

BIANCA
Is it for him you do envy me so?
Nay then you jest, and now I well perceive
You have but jested with me all this while.   20
I prithee, sister Kate, untie my hands.

tracks 5-6

8-36:
Norman Tyrrell as Baptista, Sian Phillips as Katherina, and Doria Noar as Bianca

Sirine Saba as Katherina and Sheridan Smith as Bianca in Regent Park's Open Air Theatre 2006 production directed by Rachel Kavanaugh
Photo: Donald Cooper

23: **dame**: madam (as a term of rebuke)
26: **hilding**: vicious beast
29: **flouts**: mocks, insults

30: Stage Direction: ***Exit [BIANCA]***: Bianca's name is not in the First Folio; Rowe (1709) first inserted it.

31: **suffer me**: let me have my own way
33–34: **I must...hell**: two traditional or proverbial fates of old maids

36: Stage Direction: ***[Exit]***: not in the First Folio; Rowe (1709) first inserted it
38: Stage Direction: ***Enter GREMIO...and books.***: The First Folio omits Hortensio altogether and does not name Biondello; Rowe (1709) inserted both names; ***mean***: lower-class

KATHERINA
If that be jest, then all the rest was so.
                                    Strikes her. Enter BAPTISTA.

BAPTISTA
Why how now, dame, whence grows this insolence?
Bianca, stand aside. Poor girl, she weeps.
Go ply thy needle; meddle not with her.   25
For shame, thou hilding of a devilish spirit,
Why dost thou wrong her that did ne'er wrong thee?
When did she cross thee with a bitter word?

KATHERINA
Her silence flouts me, and I'll be revenged.
                                    Flies after BIANCA

BAPTISTA
What, in my sight? Bianca, get thee in.   30
                                    Exit [BIANCA]

KATHERINA
What, will you not suffer me? Nay, now I see
She is your treasure, she must have a husband;
I must dance bare-foot on her wedding day,
And for your love to her, lead apes in hell.
Talk not to me. I will go sit and weep,   35
Till I can find occasion of revenge.
                                    [Exit]

BAPTISTA
Was ever gentleman thus grieved as I?
But who comes here.
                Enter GREMIO, LUCENTIO, in the habit of a mean man,
                    PETRUCHIO with [HORTENSIO as a musician, and]
                TRANIO, with his boy [BIONDELLO,] bearing a lute and books.

GREMIO
Good morrow, neighbor Baptista.

41–42: And you...fair and virtuous: set as prose in the First Folio; first emended to verse by Capell (1768)

44: orderly: properly, in a more orderly way

47–52: Scene: That...heard: In Jonathan Miller's 1980 BBC film, during these lines the sound of Katherina (Sarah Badel) bellowing could be heard offstage.

53: entrance...entertainment: entrance fee for my reception

55: Cunning: skilled

56: sciences: fields of knowledge

62: not for your turn: not the one for you, not right for you

64: like not of: do not like

BAPTISTA

Good morrow, neighbor Gremio. God save you, gentlemen.   40

PETRUCHIO

And you, good sir. Pray, have you not a daughter
Called Katherina, fair and virtuous?

BAPTISTA

I have a daughter, sir, called Katherina.

GREMIO

You are too blunt; go to it orderly.

PETRUCHIO

You wrong me, Signor Gremio; give me leave.   45
I am a gentleman of Verona, sir,
That hearing of her beauty and her wit,
Her affability and bashful modesty,
Her wondrous qualities, and mild behavior,
Am bold to show myself a forward guest   50
Within your house, to make mine eye the witness
Of that report, which I so oft have heard.
And for an entrance to my entertainment,
I do present you with a man of mine,
Cunning in music and the mathematics,   55
To instruct her fully in those sciences,
Whereof I know she is not ignorant.
Accept of him, or else you do me wrong.
His name is Litio, born in Mantua.

BAPTISTA

Y'are welcome, sir, and he for your good sake.   60
But for my daughter Katherine, this I know,
She is not for your turn, the more my grief.

PETRUCHIO

I see you do not mean to part with her,
Or else you like not of my company.

70–72: **Saving your...marvelous forward**: set as prose in the First Folio; first emended to verse, though divided differently, by Capell (1768) and in this division by John Stockdale (1784) **Saving**: with all respect to; *Bacare*: stand back

73: **I would...doing**: I want to get on with the business

74–80: **I doubt...his service**: set as verse in the First Folio; first emended to prose by Pope (1723-5)

74: **Neighbor**: The First Folio reads "neighbors"; Theobald (1733) first made this emendation.

75: **grateful**: welcome

77: **unto you this**: The First Folio reads "unto this"; Capell (1768) first made this emendation

BAPTISTA

    Mistake me not; I speak but as I find.   65

    Whence are you, sir? What may I call your name?

PETRUCHIO

    Petruchio is my name, Antonio's son,

    A man well known throughout all Italy.

BAPTISTA

    I know him well; you are welcome for his sake.

GREMIO

    Saving your tale, Petruchio, I pray   70

    Let us that are poor petitioners speak too.

    Bacare, you are marvelous forward.

PETRUCHIO

    Oh, pardon me, signor Gremio, I would fain be doing.

GREMIO

    I doubt it not, sir, but you will curse your wooing. Neighbor, this

    is a gift very grateful, I am sure of it. To express the like kindness   75

    myself, that have been more kindly beholding you than any, freely

    give unto you this young scholar, that hath been long studying at

    Rheims, as cunning in Greek, Latin, and other languages, as the

    other in music and mathematics. His name is Cambio; pray

    accept his service.   80

BAPTISTA

    A thousand thanks, Signor Gremio. Welcome, good Cambio. But,

    gentle sir, methinks you walk like a stranger. May I be so bold, to

    know the cause of your coming?

TRANIO

    Pardon me, sir, the boldness is mine own,

    That being a stranger in this city here,   85

    Do make myself a suitor to your daughter,

    Unto Bianca, fair and virtuous.

    Nor is your firm resolve unknown to me,

Set design from the Oregon Shakespeare Festival's 1991 production directed
by Sandy McCallum
Set Design: Michael Ganio. Courtesy of the Oregon Shakespeare Festival

89: **the preferment of**: giving precedence to

101: Stage Direction: **[*To HORTENSIO*]...[*To LUCENTIO*]**: These directions are not in the
First Folio; Capell (1768) indicates these directions with symbols, and Malone (1790)
makes the full emendation.

106: Stage Direction: **[*Exit Servant, HORTENSIO, and LUCENTIO*]**: This direction is not
in the First Folio; Capell (1768) first added it and included Biondello.

110: **asketh**: demands, requires

In the preferment of the eldest sister.
This liberty is all that I request,   90
That upon knowledge of my parentage,
I may have welcome 'mongst the rest that woo,
And free access and favor as the rest.
And toward the education of your daughters
I here bestow a simple instrument   95
And this small packet of Greek and Latin books.
If you accept them, then their worth is great.

BAPTISTA
Lucentio is your name. Of whence I pray?

TRANIO
Of Pisa, sir, son to Vincentio.

BAPTISTA
A mighty man of Pisa. By report   100
I know him well. You are very welcome, sir.
[*To HORTENSIO*] Take you the lute, [*To LUCENTIO*] and you the
    set of books;
You shall go see your pupils presently.
Holla, within!

                                                       Enter Servant
                    Sirrah, lead these gentlemen
To my daughters, and tell them both   105
These are their tutors. Bid them use them well.
                    [Exit Servant, HORTENSIO, and LUCENTIO]
We will go walk a little in the orchard,
And then to dinner. You are passing welcome,
And so I pray you all to think yourselves.

PETRUCHIO
Signor Baptista, my business asketh haste,   110
And every day I cannot come to woo.
You knew my father well, and in him me,
Left solely heir to all his lands and goods,
Which I have bettered rather than decreased.

118: **in possession**: i.e., in your immediate possession

120: **Her widowhood**: i.e., the estate provided to her as a widow

122: **Let...between us**: let precise contracts be drawn up between us

134: **happy be thy speed**: good luck to you

136: **to the proof**: to the point of invulnerability

137: Stage Direction: ***broke***: injured, bleeding. Many productions have had Hortensio enter with the lute broken over his head. However, as Patrick Tucker has pointed out (*Secrets of Acting Shakespeare*, 2002), it is funnier if Hortensio merely enters bleeding or bandaged and the explanation comes later (2.1.144) because the mental image of "a head going through a lute is funnier than the reality".

Then tell me, if I get your daughter's love,   115
What dowry shall I have with her to wife?

BAPTISTA
After my death, the one half of my lands,
And in possession twenty thousand crowns.

PETRUCHIO
And for that dowry, I'll assure her of
Her widowhood, be it that she survive me,   120
In all my lands and leases whatsoever.
Let specialties be therefore drawn between us,
That covenants may be kept on either hand.

BAPTISTA
Ay, when the special thing is well obtained,
That is, her love, for that is all in all.   125

PETRUCHIO
Why, that is nothing, for I tell you, father,
I am as peremptory as she proud minded;
And where two raging fires meet together,
They do consume the thing that feeds their fury.
Though little fire grows great with little wind,   130
Yet extreme gusts will blow out fire and all.
So I to her, and so she yields to me,
For I am rough, and woo not like a babe.

BAPTISTA
Well may'st thou woo, and happy be thy speed.
But be thou armed for some unhappy words.   135

PETRUCHIO
Ay, to the proof, as mountains are for winds,
That shakes not, though they blow perpetually.
                              Enter HORTENSIO with his head broke

BAPTISTA
How now, my friend, why dost thou look so pale?

140: Scene: **What...musician**: During this line in Jonathan Miller's 1980 BBC film the lute was thrown in to hit Hortensio (Jonathan Cecil).

142: **hold with her**: withstand her, remain unbroken by her

143: **break**: train

145: **frets**: bars on the fingerboard of a lute or guitar. Later (2.1.148), the word is used to mean vexations.

148: **fume**: show anger, rage

154: **twangling**: playing lightly or in a trifling manner; **Jack**: base or silly fellow

156: **lusty**: spirited, full of life

161: **apt**: ready, willing

HORTENSIO
For fear, I promise you, if I look pale.

BAPTISTA
What, will my daughter prove a good musician?   140

HORTENSIO
I think she'll sooner prove a soldier.
Iron may hold with her, but never lutes.

BAPTISTA
Why then thou canst not break her to the lute?

HORTENSIO
Why no, for she hath broke the lute to me.
I did but tell her she mistook her frets,   145
And bowed her hand to teach her fingering,
When, with a most impatient devilish spirit,
"Frets, call you these?" quoth she, "I'll fume with them."
And with that word she struck me on the head,
And through the instrument my pate made way,   150
And there I stood amazèd for a while,
As on a pillory, looking through the lute,
While she did call me "rascal fiddler,"
And "twangling Jack," with twenty such vile terms,
As had she studied to misuse me so.   155

PETRUCHIO
Now, by the world, it is a lusty wench.
I love her ten times more than e'er I did.
Oh, how I long to have some chat with her!

BAPTISTA
Well, go with me, and be not so discomfited.
Proceed in practice with my younger daughter;   160
She's apt to learn, and thankful for good turns.
Signor Petruchio, will you go with us,
Or shall I send my daughter Kate to you?

164: Stage Direction: *[Exeunt.] Manet PETRUCHIO.*: In the First Folio, the stage direction appears after line 162 (i.e., two lines earlier) and *"Exeunt"* is *"Exit"*.

164: **attend**: wait for
166: **rail**: complain, scold, protest strongly
173: **pack**: go away
175: **deny**: refuse

168–176: Scene: **Say that…married**: In Jonathan Miller's 1980 BBC film, John Cleese's gently meditative delivery of this speech is striking.

Douglas Fairbanks as Petruchio and Mary Pickford as Katherina in the 1929 film directed by Sam Taylor
Courtesy of Douglas Lanier

tracks 7-9

178-213:
Peter O'Toole as Petruchio and Sian Phillips as Katherina
Roger Allam as Petruchio and Frances Barber as Katherina

179: **heard…hard**: Both words would have been pronounced the same (as "hard"), so Katherina is punning.
182: **bonny**: fine and strong
185: **For dainties…Kates**: a pun on Katherina's name, the word "cates" means delicacies
188: **sounded**: proclaimed, also measured (as indicated in the next line)
191: **in good time**: indeed
193: **a movable**: a piece of furniture, also a changeable person

PETRUCHIO
I pray you do.

[Exeunt.] Manet PETRUCHIO.

I'll attend her here,
And woo her with some spirit when she comes.   165
Say that she rail, why then I'll tell her plain
She sings as sweetly as a nightingale;
Say that she frown, I'll say she looks as clear
As morning roses newly washed with dew;
Say she be mute, and will not speak a word,   170
Then I'll commend her volubility,
And say she uttereth piercing eloquence;
If she do bid me pack, I'll give her thanks,
As though she bid me stay by her a week;
If she deny to wed, I'll crave the day   175
When I shall ask the banns, and when be married.
But here she comes, and now Petruchio speak.

Enter KATHERINA

Good morrow, Kate, for that's your name, I hear.

KATHERINA
Well have you heard, but something hard of hearing.
They call me Katherine that do talk of me.   180

PETRUCHIO
You lie, in faith, for you are called plain Kate,
And bonny Kate, and sometimes Kate the curst;
But Kate, the prettiest Kate in Christendom,
Kate of Kate Hall, my super-dainty Kate,
For dainties are all Kates, and therefore, Kate,   185
Take this of me, Kate of my consolation:
Hearing thy mildness praised in every town,
Thy virtues spoke of, and thy beauty sounded,
Yet not so deeply as to thee belongs,
Myself am moved to woo thee for my wife.   190

KATHERINA
"Moved," in good time! Let him that moved you hither
Remove you hence. I knew you at the first
You were a movable.

tracks 7-9

178-213:
Peter O'Toole as Petruchio and Sian Phillips as Katherina
Roger Allam as Petruchio and Frances Barber as Katherina

194: **joint stool**: wooden stool made by a joiner

195: "Asses are made to bear, and so are you": Flora Montgomery as Katherina and Richard
Dillane as Petruchio in the Bristol Old Vic 2006 production directed by Anne Tipton
Photo: Donald Cooper

195: **bear**: carry loads
196: **bear**: 1) bear children, and 2) bear the weight of a man (in a sexual sense)
198: **burden**: 1) make accusations against, and 2) weigh heavily on
199: **light**: 1) light in weight, and 2) promiscuous
200: **light**: quick in intelligence
201: **heavy...weight**: financially sound
202: **be...buzz**: Petruchio puns on "be" / "bee" and therefore buzzes; "buzz" has also
implied "rumor," possibly introducing the issue of Katherina's reputation; **a buzzard**:
a reference to an inferior hunting bird meaning a useless, stupid person, or a drone
203: **turtle**: i.e., turtle-dove (proverbial for faithful love); **buzzard**: bird of prey
204: **Ay...buzzard**: This difficult line has inspired complicated editorial explanations.
H. J. Oliver (1982) offers this: "if a fool of a buzzard takes me, thinking me to be a turtle-dove, he is making a bad miscalculation, as the turtle-dove is mistaken when it
catches the insect known as a buzzard (presumably not to the turtle's taste)." The
transition from this insect to the next line's wasp (2.1.205) and thus to Katherina's
waspish nature is an easy one.

PETRUCHIO
                    Why, what's a movable?

KATHERINA
  A joint stool.

PETRUCHIO
              Thou hast hit it; come, sit on me.

KATHERINA
  Asses are made to bear, and so are you.   195

PETRUCHIO
  Women are made to bear, and so are you.

KATHERINA
  No such jade as you, if me you mean.

PETRUCHIO
  Alas, good Kate, I will not burden thee,
  For knowing thee to be but young and light.

KATHERINA
  Too light for such a swain as you to catch,   200
  And yet as heavy as my weight should be.

PETRUCHIO
  Should be? Should—buzz!

KATHERINA
                    Well ta'en, and like a buzzard.

PETRUCHIO
  Oh slow-winged turtle, shall a buzzard take thee?

KATHERINA
  Ay, for a turtle, as he takes a buzzard.

PETRUCHIO
  Come, come, you wasp, i' faith you are too angry.   205

178-213:
Peter O'Toole as Petruchio and Sian Phillips as Katherina
Roger Allam as Petruchio and Frances Barber as Katherina

209: "Who knows not where a wasp does wear his sting?":
Elizabeth Taylor as Kate and Richard Burton as Petruchio in the
1967 film directed by Franco Zeffirelli
© 1967 Columbia Pictures Corporation, Courtesy of Douglas Lanier

210–212: **Whose tongue?...your tail?**: Thomas Bowdler's *Family Shakespeare* (1818) omits this bawdy exchange, no doubt in pursuit of the title-page's assurance that "those words and expressions are omitted which cannot with propriety be read aloud in a family."

212: Scene: **What...tail?**: This line often receives a shocked response from Katherina or is cut altogether on the grounds of obscenity. However, in Doran's 2003 RSC production, Katherina (Alexandra Gilbreath) laughed uproariously. By contrast, Fiona Shaw (Miller's 1987 RSC production) felt that Katherina was appalled by the obscenity and so walloped Petruchio at 213: "That slap is the first clue that Kate's behaviour is, ironically, a plea for dignity."

212–213: **What with...a gentleman**: Lines divide after "your taile" in the First Folio.
213: **try**: test
215: **lose your arms**: 1) lose your right to a coat of arms, and also 2) let go
218: **A herald...books**: A herald is an official of the College of Arms, which decides who has the right to have a coat of arms and records the arms in a register. Here, there is also the sense of Petruchio wanting to be in Katherina's good books or approved by her.

KATHERINA
If I be waspish, best beware my sting.

PETRUCHIO
My remedy is then to pluck it out.

KATHERINA
Ay, if the fool could find it where it lies.

PETRUCHIO
Who knows not where a wasp does wear his sting?
In his tail.

KATHERINA
                In his tongue?

PETRUCHIO
                            Whose tongue?   210

KATHERINA
Yours, if you talk of tales, and so farewell.

PETRUCHIO
What with my tongue in your tail? Nay, come again.
Good Kate, I am a gentleman.

KATHERINA
                        That I'll try.

She strikes him

PETRUCHIO
I swear I'll cuff you if you strike again.

KATHERINA
So may you lose your arms,   215
If you strike me, you are no gentleman,
And if no gentleman, why then no arms.

PETRUCHIO
A herald, Kate? Oh, put me in thy books.

219: **crest**: 1) figure or device borne above the shield and helmet in a coat of arms, also 2) a tuft of feathers on a bird's head; **coxcomb**: fool's hat (so named because it resembled a cock's comb in shape and color)

221: **craven**: coward, one who gives up too easily

221: Scene: **No...craven**: In Jonathan Miller's 1980 BBC film Petruchio (John Cleese) made the sound of a chicken clucking; he did so again at later points in the play (such as 2.1.279 and 4.1.113).

223: **crab**: 1) i.e., crab-apple (which is very sour), also 2) sour-looking or sour-tempered person

226: **glass**: mirror

227: **Well...one**: a good hit for someone so inexperienced

KATHERINA
What is your crest, a coxcomb?

PETRUCHIO
A combless cock, so Kate will be my hen.   220

KATHERINA
No cock of mine, you crow too like a craven.

PETRUCHIO
Nay, come, Kate, come; you must not look so sour.

KATHERINA
It is my fashion when I see a crab.

PETRUCHIO
Why here's no crab, and therefore look not sour.

KATHERINA
There is, there is.   225

PETRUCHIO
Then show it me.

KATHERINA
                    Had I a glass, I would.

PETRUCHIO
What, you mean my face?

KATHERINA
                    Well aimed of such a young one.

PETRUCHIO
Now, by Saint George, I am too young for you.

KATHERINA
Yet you are withered.

230: 'scape: escape
231: **chafe**: irritate; also, possibly, excite; **tarry**: linger
232: **passing**: very
233: **coy**: distant, disdainful
234: **very**: utter
235: **gamesome**: playful, merry
237: **askance**: scornfully
239: **cross**: quarrelsome, disagreeable
241: **conference**: conversation

242: Scene: **Why...limp?**: Because of this line Jude Kelly's 1993 production for the West Yorkshire Playhouse had a disabled Kate (Nichola McAuliffe) limping and wearing a surgical boot.

246: **halt**: limp
247: **whom...command**: boss your servants around
248–251: Scene: **Did ever...sportful**: In Jonathan Miller's 1980 BBC film, Petruchio (John Cleese) delivered these lines in an artificial voice and with exaggeratedly expansive gestures, as if parodying an over-the-top actor.

251: "Go, fool, and whom thou keep'st command": Amy van Nostrand as Katherina and Jonathan Epstein as Petruchio in the Shakespeare Theatre Company's 1994-1995 production directed by Adrian Hall
Photo: Carol Pratt

250: **Diana**: Diana, goddess of chastity and hunting
251: **sportful**: amorous, frolicsome

PETRUCHIO
                'Tis with cares.

KATHERINA
                              I care not.

PETRUCHIO
  Nay hear you, Kate. In sooth you 'scape not so.   230

KATHERINA
  I chafe you if I tarry. Let me go.

PETRUCHIO
  No, not a whit. I find you passing gentle.
  'Twas told me you were rough, and coy, and sullen,
  And now I find report a very liar,
  For thou art pleasant, gamesome, passing courteous,   235
  But slow in speech, yet sweet as spring-time flowers.
  Thou canst not frown, thou canst not look askance,
  Nor bite the lip, as angry wenches will,
  Nor hast thou pleasure to be cross in talk;
  But thou with mildness entertain'st thy wooers,   240
  With gentle conference, soft and affable.
  Why does the world report that Kate doth limp?
  Oh, sland'rous world! Kate, like the hazel twig,
  Is straight and slender, and as brown in hue
  As hazel nuts, and sweeter than the kernels.   245
  Oh, let me see thee walk. Thou dost not halt.

KATHERINA
  Go, fool, and whom thou keep'st command.

PETRUCHIO
  Did ever Dian so become a grove
  As Kate this chamber with her princely gate?
  Oh, be thou Dian, and let her be Kate,   250
  And then let Kate be chaste, and Dian sportful.

KATHERINA
  Where did you study all this goodly speech?

253: **mother wit**: natural intelligence or inborn wit

255: **keep you warm**: an insulting allusion to the proverb "He is wise enough that can keep himself warm"

260: **will you, nill you**: whether you like it or not

261: **for your turn**: to suit you

264: Stage Direction: ***Enter BAPTISTA, GREMIO, [and] TRANIO***: This direction follows line 264 in the First Folio, but most editors have it follow line 265. However, Patrick Tucker's argument (*Secrets of Acting Shakespeare*, 2002) that all of the last five lines of this speech are meant to be overheard by Baptista and the others (partly signaled by the change from "thou" to "you") is compelling. (In Shakespeare's time, "thou" is the more intimate term; "you" is more formal.)

264: Scene: ***Enter BAPTISTA, GREMIO, [and] TRANIO***: Commenting on the performance aspects of this entrance, Alan Dessen writes, "The earlier entry, especially if Petruchio is immediately aware of the observers, provides some rich comic possibilities" (*Recovering Shakespeare's*, 68). In Doran's 2003 RSC production Baptista and the others entered here and Petruchio's tone, which had been quite tender, changed to an aggressive bellow with "For I am he am born to tame you, Kate", which was clearly for the other men's benefit.

tracks 10-12

265-313: *Roger Allam as Petruchio, Sean Baker as Baptista, Frances Barber as Katherina, and Ensemble*
Marc Singer as Petruchio, William Paterson as Baptista, Fredi Olster as Katherina, and Ensemble

269: Scene: **I must...wife**: In Gale Edwards' 1995 RSC production when Baptista (Clifford Rose) and the others re-entered during this line, Petruchio (Michael Siberry) and Katherina (Josie Lawrence) were rolling on the ground fighting, so Baptista's question (2.1.270) was very comical. This staging and Petruchio's reply (2.1.271–2) made the audience laugh. In Taichman's 2007 Shakespeare Theatre Company Production in Washington, DC Katherina (Charlayne Woodard) bit Petruchio (Christopher Innvar).

270: **how speed you with my daughter?**: i.e., how do you get on with my daughter?

273: **in your dumps**: down in the dumps, miserable, depressed

PETRUCHIO
It is extempore, from my mother wit.

KATHERINA
A witty mother, witless else her son.

PETRUCHIO
Am I not wise?

KATHERINA
                        Yes, keep you warm.   255

PETRUCHIO
Marry, so I mean, sweet Katherine, in thy bed.
And therefore, setting all this chat aside,
Thus in plain terms: your father hath consented
That you shall be my wife, your dowry 'greed on,
And will you, nill you, I will marry you.   260
Now, Kate, I am a husband for your turn,
For by this light, whereby I see thy beauty,
Thy beauty that doth make me like thee well,
Thou must be married to no man but me,
                        Enter BAPTISTA, GREMIO, [and] TRANIO
For I am he am born to tame you, Kate,   265
And bring you from a wild Kate to a Kate
Conformable as other household Kates.
Here comes your father. Never make denial;
I must and will have Katherine to my wife.

BAPTISTA
Now, Signor Petruchio, how speed you with my daughter?   270

PETRUCHIO
How but well, sir? How but well?
It were impossible I should speed amiss.

BAPTISTA
Why, how now, daughter Katherine, in your dumps?

265-313: *Roger Allam as Petruchio, Sean Baker as Baptista, Frances Barber as Katherina, and Ensemble*
Marc Singer as Petruchio, William Paterson as Baptista, Fredi Olster as Katherina, and Ensemble

tracks 10-12

274: **promise**: assure

278: **face**: brazen

279–287: Scene: **Father...wedding day**: In Gale Edwards' 1995 RSC production, this speech was delivered by Petruchio (Michael Siberry) while he had Katherina (Josie Lawrence) tightly gripped and unable to speak or get up. She escaped and leaped to her feet to shout, "I'll see thee hanged" (2.1.288) but refused to give him her hands or to kiss him. 281: **for policy**: as a tactic

284: **Grissel**: i.e., Griselda. In Chaucer's *Clerk's Tale* and elsewhere, Patient Griselda is the model of a patient wife, the opposite of a shrew.

285: **Lucrece**: The model chaste wife Lucrece, whose story has appeared in many versions including Shakespeare's long poem *The Rape of Lucrece* (1594), committed suicide after being raped by Tarquin.

Bebe Neuwirth as Katherina and Roger Rees as Petruchio in the 1999 Williamstown Theatre Festival production directed by Roger Rees
Photo: Richard Feldman. Courtesy of Williamstown Theatre Festival

290: **speeding**: success; **goodnight our part**: say goodnight (goodbye) to our plans

293: **twixt us twain**: between the two of us

298: **vied**: redoubled, repeated

299: **twink**: the twinkling of an eye, i.e., instantaneously

300: **a world**: worth a world

KATHERINA
    Call you me daughter? Now I promise you
    You have showed a tender fatherly regard   275
    To wish me wed to one half lunatic,
    A mad-cap ruffian and a swearing Jack,
    That thinks with oaths to face the matter out.

PETRUCHIO
    Father, 'tis thus: yourself and all the world
    That talked of her have talked amiss of her.   280
    If she be curst, it is for policy,
    For she's not froward, but modest as the dove;
    She is not hot, but temperate as the morn;
    For patience she will prove a second Grissel,
    And Roman Lucrece for her chastity.   285
    And, to conclude, we have 'greed so well together
    That upon Sunday is the wedding day.

KATHERINA
    I'll see thee hanged on Sunday first.

GREMIO
    Hark, Petruchio, she says she'll see thee hanged first.

TRANIO
    Is this your speeding? Nay then goodnight our part.   290

PETRUCHIO
    Be patient, gentlemen, I choose her for myself.
    If she and I be pleased, what's that to you?
    'Tis bargained twixt us twain being alone,
    That she shall still be curst in company.
    I tell you 'tis incredible to believe   295
    How much she loves me. Oh, the kindest Kate,
    She hung about my neck, and kiss on kiss
    She vied so fast, protesting oath on oath,
    That in a twink she won me to her love.
    Oh, you are novices. 'Tis a world to see   300
    How tame, when men and women are alone,

tracks 10-12

265-313: *Roger Allam as Petruchio, Sean Baker as Baptista, Frances Barber as Katherina, and Ensemble*
Marc Singer as Petruchio, William Paterson as Baptista, Fredi Olster as Katherina, and Ensemble

302: **meacock**: weakling, spiritless

303–306: Scene: **Give me...fine**: In Jonathan Miller's 1980 BBC film Petruchio (John Cleese) grabbed Katherina's hand and during the rest of these lines he held both of her arms hard against her body so that she could not move.

304: **'gainst**: ready for

311-312: "I will to Venice; Sunday comes apace. / We will have rings, and things, and fine array":
Richard Burton as Petruchio and ensemble in the 1967 film directed by Franco Zeffirelli
Copyright © 1967 Columbia Pictures Corporation, Courtesy of Douglas Lanier

313: Scene: **kiss me...Sunday**: In Lindsay Posner's 1999 RSC production Petruchio (Stuart McQuarrie) bent Katherina (Monica Dolan) over his arm and kissed her; when he let go, she fell to the floor. After Petruchio exited, Katherina got up and spat in Baptista's face.

314: **clapped up**: arranged hastily

316: **desperate mart**: risky business venture

317: **'Twas...you**: the commodity (Katherina) was becoming less valuable as it remained unsold

319: **quiet in**: The First Folio reads "quiet me"; Rowe (1714) first made this emendation.

A meacock wretch can make the curstest shrew.
Give me thy hand, Kate, I will unto Venice
To buy apparel 'gainst the wedding day.
Provide the feast, Father, and bid the guests.   305
I will be sure my Katherine shall be fine.

BAPTISTA

I know not what to say, but give me your hands.
God send you joy, Petruchio; 'tis a match.

GREMIO and TRANIO

Amen say we, we will be witnesses.

PETRUCHIO

Father, and wife, and gentlemen, adieu.   310
I will to Venice; Sunday comes apace.
We will have rings, and things, and fine array,
And kiss me, Kate, we will be married a' Sunday.
                    Exeunt PETRUCHIO and KATHERINA

GREMIO

Was ever match clapped up so suddenly?

BAPTISTA

Faith, gentlemen, now I play a merchant's part,   315
And venture madly on a desperate mart.

TRANIO

'Twas a commodity lay fretting by you;
'Twill bring you gain, or perish on the seas.

BAPTISTA

The gain I seek is quiet in the match.

GREMIO

No doubt but he hath got a quiet catch.   320
But now, Baptista, to your younger daughter;
Now is the day we long have lookèd for,
I am your neighbor, and was suitor first.

326: **Youngling**: youngster, inexperienced person

328: **Skipper**: contemptuous term for a young, irresponsible person

332: **dower**: the counterpart of dowry, this is the settlement of property on the wife by the husband

335–387: Scene: **First, as...thank you both**: In Taichman's 2007 Shakespeare Theatre Company Production in Washington, DC, the scene was set as an auction with Baptista (Nicholas Hormann) at a podium and all three with microphones.

336: **plate and gold**: utensils of silver and gold

337: **lave**: wash

338: **hangings**: 1) wall coverings and 2) bed curtains; **Tyrian**: purple

339: **coffers**: chests, boxes

340: **arras counterpoints**: counterpanes of Arras tapestry

341: **tents**: bed canopies

342: **bossed**: ornamented, embossed

343: **Venice...needlework**: Venetian embroidery in gold thread

346: **milch-kine...pail**: cows whose milk is sold for human consumption

TRANIO
    And I am one that love Bianca more
    Than words can witness, or your thoughts can guess.   325

GREMIO
    Youngling, thou canst not love so dear as I.

TRANIO
    Graybeard, thy love doth freeze.

GREMIO
                           But thine doth fry.
    Skipper, stand back. 'Tis age that nourisheth.

TRANIO
    But youth in ladies' eyes that flourisheth.

BAPTISTA
    Content you, gentlemen. I will compound this strife.   330
    'Tis deeds must win the prize, and he of both
    That can assure my daughter greatest dower
    Shall have my Bianca's love.
    Say, Signor Gremio, what can you assure her?

GREMIO
    First, as you know, my house within the city   335
    Is richly furnishèd with plate and gold,
    Basins and ewers to lave her dainty hands;
    My hangings all of Tyrian tapestry;
    In ivory coffers I have stuffed my crowns;
    In cypress chests my arras counterpoints,   340
    Costly apparel, tents, and canopies,
    Fine linen, Turkey cushions bossed with pearl,
    Valance of Venice gold, in needlework,
    Pewter and brass, and all things that belongs
    To house or housekeeping. Then at my farm   345
    I have a hundred milch-kine to the pail,
    Six score fat oxen standing in my stalls,
    And all things answerable to this portion.

349: **struck in years**: old

352: **list**: listen

358: **ducats**: gold coins

359: **her jointure**: the estate she will inherit at his death

360: **pinched you**: put you in a tight corner

363: **argosy**: merchant vessel

364: **lying in Marcellus' road**: sheltered or anchored outside Marseilles harbor

367: **galliasses**: sea-faring vessels slightly larger than galleys (see line 368), propelled by sails and oars, and often employed in war

368: **tight**: watertight

374: **outvied**: outbid

Myself am struck in years, I must confess,
And if I die to morrow this is hers,   350
If whil'st I live she will be only mine.

TRANIO
   That "only" came well in. Sir, list to me:
   I am my father's heir and only son.
   If I may have your daughter to my wife,
   I'll leave her houses three or four as good   355
   Within rich Pisa walls, as any one
   Old Signor Gremio has in Padua,
   Besides, two thousand ducats by the year
   Of fruitful land, all which shall be her jointure.
   What, have I pinched you, Signor Gremio?   360

GREMIO
   Two thousand ducats by the year of land!
   My land amounts not to so much in all.
   That she shall have, besides an argosy
   That now is lying in Marcellus' road.
   What, have I choked you with an argosy?   365

TRANIO
   Gremio, 'tis known my father hath no less
   Than three great argosies, besides two galliasses
   And twelve tight galleys. These I will assure her,
   And twice as much what e'er thou offrest next.

GREMIO
   Nay, I have offered all. I have no more,   370
   And she can have no more than all I have.
   If you like me, she shall have me and mine.

TRANIO
   Why, then the maid is mine from all the world
   By your firm promise. Gremio is outvied.

BAPTISTA
   I must confess your offer is the best,   375
   And let your father make her the assurance,

382–383: Scene: **On Sunday...married**: In Doran's 2003 RSC production Baptista (Ian Gelder) roared with triumphant laughter when he said this. In Taichman's 2007 Shakespeare Theatre Company Production Baptista (Nicholas Hormann) made a steeple with his hands as a gesture of thankfulness.

388: Stage Direction: *Exit [BAPTISTA]*: The First Folio reads "*Exit*" and the stage direction follows line 389.

389: **gamester**: gambler

391: **Set...table**: rely on your charity; **toy**: foolish idea

394: **faced...ten**: bluffed, brazened it out

397: **get**: beget

She is your own; else, you must pardon me.
If you should die before him, where's her dower?

TRANIO
That's but a cavil. He is old, I young.

GREMIO
And may not young men die as well as old?   380

BAPTISTA
Well, gentlemen, I am thus resolved:
On Sunday next, you know
My daughter Katherine is to be married.
Now on the Sunday following shall Bianca
Be bride to you, if you make this assurance;   385
If not, to Signor Gremio.
And so I take my leave, and thank you both.

GREMIO
Adieu, good neighbor.

                                         Exit [BAPTISTA]
                    Now I fear thee not.
Sirrah, young gamester, your father were a fool
To give thee all, and in his waning age   390
Set foot under thy table. Tut, a toy!
An old Italian fox is not so kind, my boy.

                                                     Exit

TRANIO
A vengeance on your crafty withered hide!
Yet I have faced it with a card of ten.
'Tis in my head to do my master good.   395
I see no reason but supposed Lucentio
Must get a father, called supposed Vincentio.
And that's a wonder. Fathers commonly
Do get their children, but in this case of wooing
A child shall get a sire, if I fail not of my cunning.   400
                                                     Exit

[The Taming of
the Shrew

Act 3
7.

0: The First Folio has "*Actus Tertia*"; Rowe first made the scene division (1709).

1: "Fiddler, forbear. You grow too forward, sir": Victor Spinetti as Hortensio, Natasha Pyne as Bianca, and Michael York as Lucentio in the 1967 film directed by Franco Zeffirelli
© 1967 Columbia Pictures Corporation, Courtesy of Douglas Lanier

6: **prerogative**: precedence
8: **lecture**: lesson
9: **Preposterous**: In Shakespeare's time, preposterous meant "out of order" or "in reverse order", but this usage is rare today.
10: **ordained**: instituted
12: **usual pain**: usual labor
14: **serve in**: serve up, present
15: **braves**: insults
18: **breeching scholar in the schools**: young scholar liable to be whipped
19: **'pointed**: appointed
22: **the whiles**: for the time being, meanwhile

Act 3, Scene 1]

Enter LUCENTIO, HORTENSIO, and BIANCA

LUCENTIO
Fiddler, forbear. You grow too forward, sir.
Have you so soon forgot the entertainment
Her sister Katherine welcomed you withal?

HORTENSIO
But, wrangling pedant, this is
The patroness of heavenly harmony.   5
Then give me leave to have prerogative,
And when in music we have spent an hour,
Your lecture shall have leisure for as much.

LUCENTIO
Preposterous ass, that never read so far
To know the cause why music was ordained.   10
Was it not to refresh the mind of man
After his studies, or his usual pain?
Then give me leave to read philosophy,
And while I pause, serve in your harmony.

HORTENSIO
Sirrah, I will not bear these braves of thine.   15

BIANCA
Why, gentlemen, you do me double wrong,
To strive for that which resteth in my choice.
I am no breeching scholar in the schools;
I'll not be tied to hours, nor 'pointed times,
But learn my lessons as I please myself.   20
And to cut off all strife, here sit we down.
Take you your instrument, play you the whiles;
His lecture will be done ere you have tuned.

HORTENSIO
You'll leave his lecture when I am in tune?

27-28: "Here, madam / *Hic ibat Simois; hic est Sigeia tellus*": Michael Medico as
Lucentio and Dallas Roberts as Bianca in the Shakespeare Theatre Company's
1994-1995 production directed by Adrian Hall
Photo: Carol Pratt

28-29: *Hic ibat...celsa senis*: appears as prose in First Folio; Lewis Theobald (1733) first
set it as verse. The passage is a quotation from Ovid's *Heroides*: "Here flowed the
river Simois; here is the Sigeian land; here stood the lofty palace of old Priam."

28, 32, 40: *Sigeia*: The First Folio reads *"sigeria"*; the Second Folio (1632) makes these
corrections.

30: **Conster**: translate, construe

34: **port**: social position, style

31–35: Scene: *Hic ibat...pantaloon*: In Jonathan Miller's 1980 BBC film, Lucentio's
(Simon Chandler) arm was creeping gradually round the shoulder of Bianca (Susan
Penhaligon) until it was almost in her cleavage; it was removed with great rapidity
when Hortensio approached.

40: *steterat*: The First Folio reads *"staterat"*; the Second Folio (1632) makes the correction.

LUCENTIO
That will be never. Tune your instrument.   25

BIANCA
Where left we last?

LUCENTIO
Here, Madam.
Hic ibat Simois, hic est Sigeia tellus,
Hic steterat Priami regia celsa senis.

BIANCA
Conster them.   30

LUCENTIO
Hic ibat, as I told you before, *Simois*, I am Lucentio, *hic est*, son
unto Vincentio of Pisa, *Sigeia tellus*, dignified thus to get your
love, *Hic steterat*, and that Lucentio that comes a-wooing,
Priami, is my man Tranio, *regia*, bearing my port, *celsa senis*, that
we might beguile the old pantaloon.   35

HORTENSIO
Madam, my instrument's in tune.

BIANCA
Let's hear. Oh fie, the treble jars.

LUCENTIO
Spit in the hole, man, and tune again.

BIANCA
Now let me see if I can conster it. *Hic ibat Simois*, I know you
not, *hic est Sigeia tellus*, I trust you not, *hic steterat Priami*, take   40
heed he hear us not, *regia*, presume not, *celsa senis*, despair not.

HORTENSIO
Madam, 'tis now in tune.

LUCENTIO
                    All but the bass.

43–54: The First Folio assigns lines 44–46 to Lucentio, 48–49 to Bianca and 50–54 to Hortensio. Pope's second edition (1728) first reassigned the lines, and Theobald first explained the "manifest *Transposition*" and recommended the change in the appendix to his *Shakespeare Restored* (1726).

44: Stage Direction: [*Aside*]: not in the First Folio; first indicated by Capell (1768)

46: **Pedascule**: contemptuous, diminutive term for pedant invented by Shakespeare

48–9: **Aeacides...grandfather**: For Hortensio's benefit, Lucentio is pretending to explain the next bit of Ovid. Ajax was also known as Aeacides, derived from the name of his grandfather, Aeacus.

54: **pleasant**: merry

55: **give me leave**: leave me alone

56: **in three parts**: for three voices

57: **formal**: punctilious, precise

58: Stage Direction: [*Aside*]: not in the First Folio; emendation first made by Samuel Johnson (1765)

58: **but**: unless

61: **order**: system, method

63: **gamut**: musical scale

HORTENSIO
  The bass is right; 'tis the base knave that jars.
  [*Aside*] How fiery and forward our pedant is.
  Now, for my life, the knave doth court my love.   45
  Pedascule, I'll watch you better yet.

BIANCA
  In time I may believe, yet I mistrust.

LUCENTIO
  Mistrust it not, for sure Aeacides
  Was Ajax, called so from his grandfather.

BIANCA
  I must believe my master; else, I promise you,   50
  I should be arguing still upon that doubt.
  But let it rest. Now, Litio, to you.
  Good master, take it not unkindly, pray,
  That I have been thus pleasant with you both.

HORTENSIO
  You may go walk, and give me leave a while;   55
  My lessons make no music in three parts.

LUCENTIO
  Are you so formal, sir? Well, I must wait
  [*Aside*] And watch withal, for, but I be deceived,
  Our fine musician groweth amorous.

HORTENSIO
  Madam, before you touch the instrument   60
  To learn the order of my fingering,
  I must begin with rudiments of art,
  To teach you gamut in a briefer sort,
  More pleasant, pithy, and effectual,
  Than hath been taught by any of my trade.   65
  And there it is in writing fairly drawn.

BIANCA
  Why, I am past my gamut long ago.

Mark Rylance as Lucentio, Alice Krige as Bianca, and Ian Talbot as Hortensio in the Royal Shakespeare Company's 1982 production directed by Barry Kyle
Photo: Donald Cooper

69: Stage Direction: **[*Reads*]**: not in the First Folio; Pope (1723-25) first added the direction "*reading*".

70–74: *A re...die*: The notes A, B, C, D, E are sung "re", "mi", "fa", "sol", and "la" in the scale based on G; the scale based on C begins "ut", "re,", "mi".
70: *A re*: The First Folio reads "Are"; the 1631 quarto first makes this emendation.
71: *B mi*: The First Folio reads "Beeme"; Pope (1723-25) first made this emendation first.
72: *C fa ut*: The First Folio reads "Cfavt"; the 1631 quarto first makes this emendation.
74: *E la mi*: The First Folio reads "Ela mi"; Johnson (1765) first made this emendation.
76: **nice**: capricious
77: **change**: The First Folio reads "charge"; the Second Folio (1632) makes this emendation; **odd**: The First Folio reads "old"; Theobald (1733) first made this emendation.

77: Stage Direction: **[*SERVANT*]**: The First Folio reads "*Messenger*"; Rowe first made this emendation in 1709.
78: Speech Prefix: **SERVANT**: The First Folio reads "Nicke"; Rowe first made this emendation in 1709.
81: Stage Direction: **[*Exeunt BIANCA and SERVANT*]**: not in the First Folio; emendation first made by Capell (1768)
82: Stage Direction: **[*Exit*]**: not in the First Folio; emendation first made by Rowe in 1709

86: **stale**: lure, decoy
87: **Seize thee that list**: let anyone who wants you have you; **ranging**: inconstant, straying

HORTENSIO
    Yet read the gamut of Hortensio.

BIANCA
    [*Reads*] "*Gamut* I am, the ground of all accord:
    A re, to plead Hortensio's passion;   70
    B mi, Bianca take him for thy Lord,
    C fa ut, that loves with all affection.
    D sol re, one clef, two notes have I,
    E la mi, show pity or I die."
    Call you this gamut? Tut, I like it not.   75
    Old fashions please me best; I am not so nice
    To change true rules for odd inventions.
                                            Enter a [SERVANT]

SERVANT
    Mistress, your father prays you leave your books,
    And help to dress your sister's chamber up.
    You know tomorrow is the wedding day.   80

BIANCA
    Farewell, sweet masters both; I must be gone.
                                [Exeunt BIANCA and SERVANT]

LUCENTIO
    Faith, mistress, then I have no cause to stay.
                                                            [Exit]

HORTENSIO
    But I have cause to pry into this pedant.
    Methinks he looks as though he were in love.
    Yet if thy thoughts, Bianca, be so humble   85
    To cast thy wand'ring eyes on every stale,
    Seize thee that list. If once I find thee ranging,
    Hortensio will be quit with thee by changing.
                                                            Exit

0: There is no scene division in the First Folio; Pope first made the division (1723-5).
0: Stage Direction: *[LUCENTIO]*: The First Folio omits Lucentio; Rowe (1709) first made this emendation.

tracks 13-15

1–55: *Sean Baker as Baptista, Frances Barber as Katherina, Clarence Smith as Tranio, and Richard Pearce as Biondello*
Norman Tyrrell as Baptista, Sian Phillips as Katherina, Harry Locke as Tranio, and John Davidson as Biondello

Amy van Nostrand as Katherina, Dallas Roberts as Bianca, and attendants in the 1994-1995 Shakespeare Theatre Company production directed by Adrian Hall
Photo: Carol Pratt

5: **want**: lack

10: **rudesby**: unmannerly fellow; **spleen**: changeable temper

12: **frantic**: insane

13: **blunt**: rude

Act 3, Scene 2]

Enter BAPTISTA, GREMIO, TRANIO, KATHERINA, BIANCA,
[LUCENTIO] and others, attendants

BAPTISTA
  Signor Lucentio, this is the 'pointed day
  That Katherine and Petruchio should be married,
  And yet we hear not of our son in law.
  What will be said? What mockery will it be
  To want the bridegroom when the priest attends   5
  To speak the ceremonial rites of marriage?
  What says Lucentio to this shame of ours?

KATHERINA
  No shame but mine. I must forsooth be forced
  To give my hand opposed against my heart
  Unto a mad-brain rudesby, full of spleen,   10
  Who wooed in haste, and means to wed at leisure.
  I told you, I, he was a frantic fool,
  Hiding his bitter jests in blunt behavior.
  And to be noted for a merry man,
  He'll woo a thousand, 'point the day of marriage,   15
  Make friends, invite, and proclaim the banns,
  Yet never means to wed where he hath wooed.
  Now must the world point at poor Katherine,
  And say, "Lo, there is mad Petruchio's wife,
  If it would please him come and marry her."   20

TRANIO
  Patience, good Katherine and Baptista too.
  Upon my life Petruchio means but well,
  Whatever fortune stays him from his word.
  Though he be blunt, I know him passing wise;
  Though he be merry, yet withal he's honest.   25

KATHERINA
  Would Katherine had never seen him, though.

                                Exit weeping

1–55: *Sean Baker as Baptista, Frances Barber as Katherina, Clarence Smith as Tranio, and Richard Pearce as Biondello*
Norman Tyrrell as Baptista, Sian Phillips as Katherina, Harry Locke as Tranio, and John Davidson as Biondello

29: **thy impatient:** The First Folio lacks "thy"; the Second Folio (1632) emends the omission..

30: **old news:** The First Folio lacks "old"; John Payne Collier first made this emendation in 1842–4.

32: **hear:** The First Folio reads "heard"; the 1631 quarto makes this emendation.

40–55: Scene: **Why, Petruchio...packthread:** Much of this passage may be cut, but Petruchio's appearance when he is eventually seen (3.2.76) is an occasion for an extravagantly bizarre costume. Fiona Shaw (Katherina in Miller's 1987 RSC production) has commented: "It isn't merely comic; Kate ought to see a man dressed like a maniac. Petruchio is undermining the values of her society, and she ought to see that too. His costume should be monstrous, insulting, threatening—and a mirror for Kate to see herself in" (*Clamororus Voices*). In Taichman's 2007 Shakespeare Theatre Company Production Petruchio (Christopher Innvar) was indeed a mirror, wearing a wedding dress like Katherina's.

40: **jerkin:** short jacket

41: **thrice turned:** i.e., turned around and inside out to get more wear out of them

41–42: **boots that have been candle-cases:** boots so worn out that they have been used to store candles

BAPTISTA

    Go, girl, I cannot blame thee now to weep,
    For such an injury would vex a very saint,
    Much more a shrew of thy impatient humor.

                            Enter BIONDELLO

BIONDELLO

    Master, master, news! And such old news as you never heard of.   30

BAPTISTA

    Is it new and old too? How may that be?

BIONDELLO

    Why, is it not news to hear of Petruchio's coming?

BAPTISTA

    Is he come?

BIONDELLO

    Why, no, sir.

BAPTISTA

    What then?   35

BIONDELLO

    He is coming.

BAPTISTA

    When will he be here?

BIONDELLO

    When he stands where I am, and sees you there.

TRANIO

    But say, what to thine old news?

BIONDELLO

    Why, Petruchio is coming in a new hat and an old jerkin; a pair of   40
    old breeches thrice turned; a pair of boots that have been candle-
    cases, one buckled, another laced; an old rusty sword ta'en out of

1–55: Sean Baker as Baptista, Frances Barber as Katherina, Clarence Smith as Tranio, and Richard Pearce as Biondello
Norman Tyrrell as Baptista, Sian Phillips as Katherina, Harry Locke as Tranio, and John Davidson as Biondello

43: **chapeless**: without a sheath

44: **points**: tagged laces used to fasten hose to doublet; **horse hipped**: lame in the hip; **mothy**: moth-eaten

45: **of no kindred**: not matching; **possessed with**: suffering from; **glanders**: disease affecting horses, symptoms include swelling around the jaw and mucous in the nostrils

46: **mose**: an error for "mourn", the mucous discharge caused by the glanders; **lampass**: disease affecting horses, symptoms include swelling in the mouth behind the front teeth

47: **fashions**: horse disease like glanders, also known as "farcy"; **windgalls**: tumors on a horse's leg; **sped with spavins**: ruined with tumors; **rayed**: disfigured or defiled

48: **yellows**: i.e., jaundice; **fives**: ailment affecting horses, indicated by swollen parotid glands, also called "the strangles"; **stark**: utterly; **staggers**: diseases affecting domestic animals, characterized by a symptomatic staggering gait

49: **begnawn with**: gnawed at by; **bots**: disease caused by a parasitical worm; **swayed**: The First Folio reads "Waid"; Thomas Hanmer (1744) first made this emendation; **shoulder-shotten**: with a dislocated shoulder

50: **near legged before**: with knock-kneed forelegs; **half-cheeked bit**: The First Folio reads "halfe-chekt"; Thomas Hanmer (1744) first made this emendation. The phrase means that the bit does not work properly because it is wrongly attached or broken; **headstall**: part of the bridle that fits around the head

51: **sheep's leather**: inferior and weaker leather; **restrained**: drawn tight

53: **girth**: leather strap going around the horse's body; **pieced**: mended; **crupper**: leather strap attached to the saddle that passes under the horse's tail; **velour**: velvet

55: **packthread**: twine, string

57: **caparisoned**: dressed, outfitted

58: **stock**: stocking; **kersey boot-hose**: coarse over-stocking

59: **list**: strip of cloth

59–60: **humor...pricked**: whim or mood incited

59–60: **humor...feather**: Editors have made many efforts to explain this obscure phrase; it appears to describe elaborate or bizarre decoration.

the town armory, with a broken hilt, and chapeless; with two
broken points; his horse hipped with an old mothy saddle, and
stirrups of no kindred; besides, possessed with the glanders, and   45
like to mose in the chine, troubled with the lampass, infected with
the fashions, full of windgalls, sped with spavins, rayed with the
yellows, past cure of the fives, stark spoiled with the staggers,
begnawn with the bots, swayed in the back, and shoulder-shotten,
near legged before, and with a half-cheeked bit and a headstall of   50
sheep's leather which, being restrained to keep him from stum-
bling, hath been often burst, and now repaired with knots; one
girth six times pieced, and a woman's crupper of velour, which
hath two letters for her name fairly set down in studs, and here
and there pieced with packthread.   55

BAPTISTA
Who comes with him?

BIONDELLO
Oh, sir, his lackey, for all the world caparisoned like the horse,
with a linen stock on one leg, and a kersey boot-hose on the other,
gartered with a red and blue list; an old hat, and the humor of
forty fancies pricked in't for a feather; a monster, a very monster   60
in apparel, and not like a Christian foot-boy or a gentleman's
lackey.

TRANIO
'Tis some odd humor pricks him to this fashion,
Yet oftentimes he goes but mean appareled.

BAPTISTA
I am glad he's come, howsoe'er he comes.   65

BIONDELLO
Why, sir, he comes not.

BAPTISTA
Didst thou not say he comes?

BIONDELLO
Who? That Petruchio came?

71: **all one**: the same thing

73: **hold**: bet

72–76: **Nay...many**: These lines are set as prose in the First Folio; Rowe set the first two lines as verse in 1714; John Payne Collier first set all five lines in verse (1842–4). The jingle's source has not been identified.

79: "And yet I come not well": Jonathan Epstein as Petruchio in the Shakespeare Theatre Company's 1994-1995 production directed by Adrian Hall
Photo: Carol Pratt

84: **Gentles**: gentlemen

85: **wherefore**: why

87: **prodigy**: wonder

BAPTISTA
Ay, that Petruchio came.

BIONDELLO
No, sir, I say his horse comes with him on his back.   70

BAPTISTA
Why, that's all one.

BIONDELLO
Nay, by St. Jamy,
I hold you a penny,
A horse and a man
Is more than one,   75
And yet not many.

Enter PETRUCHIO and GRUMIO

PETRUCHIO
Come, where be these gallants? Who's at home?

BAPTISTA
You are welcome, sir.

PETRUCHIO
And yet I come not well.

BAPTISTA
And yet you halt not.   80

TRANIO
Not so well apparelled as I wish you were.

PETRUCHIO
Were it better I should rush in thus.
But where is Kate? Where is my lovely bride?
How does my father? Gentles, methinks you frown,
And wherefore gaze this goodly company,   85
As if they saw some wondrous monument,
Some comet, or unusual prodigy?

90: **unprovided**: ill equipped, unprepared

91: **doff**: take off; **estate**: status, position

93: **import**: importance

Douglas Fairbanks as Petruchio in the 1929 film directed by Sam Taylor
Courtesy of Douglas Lanier

98: **digress**: deviate, go off course

102: **wears**: progresses, is passing

103: **unreverent**: disrespectful

107: **Good sooth**: yes indeed; **ha'**: have

109: **wear**: wear out (generally regarded as a bawdy reference)

BAPTISTA

    Why, sir, you know this is your wedding day.
    First were we sad, fearing you would not come,
    Now sadder that you come so unprovided.   90
    Fie, doff this habit, shame to your estate,
    An eyesore to our solemn festival.

TRANIO

    And tell us what occasion of import
    Hath all so long detained you from your wife,
    And sent you hither so unlike yourself?   95

PETRUCHIO

    Tedious it were to tell, and harsh to hear.
    Sufficeth I am come to keep my word,
    Though in some part enforcèd to digress,
    Which at more leisure I will so excuse
    As you shall well be satisfied with all.   100
    But where is Kate? I stay too long from her.
    The morning wears; 'tis time we were at church.

TRANIO

    See not your bride in these unreverent robes.
    Go to my chamber; put on clothes of mine.

PETRUCHIO

    Not I, believe me; thus I'll visit her.   105

BAPTISTA

    But thus I trust you will not marry her.

PETRUCHIO

    Good sooth, even thus; therefore ha' done with words.
    To me she's married, not unto my clothes.
    Could I repair what she will wear in me,
    As I can change these poor accoutrements,   110
    'Twere well for Kate, and better for myself.
    But what a fool am I to chat with you,

114: **lovely**: loving

114: Stage Direction: ***Exeunt [PETRUCHIO and GRUMIO]***: The First Folio reads "*Exit*"; Capell (1768) added Grumio (and Biondello as well).

118: **event**: outcome

118: Stage Direction: ***Exeunt [BAPTISTA, GREMIO, BIONDELLO, attendants]***: The First Folio reads "*Exit*"; Capell (1768) adds "attendants"; and the 1863-6 Cambridge edition adds "Gremio".

119: **sir, to love**: The First Folio reads "sir, Loue"; various editors have suggested a variety of additions such as Pope ("But, Sir, our love") and Capell, but Charles Knight first made this emendation in 1839; **concerneth us**: it is necessary for us

123: **skills not**: does not matter; **turn**: purpose, need

125: **make assurance**: guarantee

131: **steal our marriage**: elope, marry secretly

135: **vantage**: opportunity, advantage

136: **over-reach**: get the better of, outdo

138: **quaint**: crafty, cunning

When I should bid good morrow to my bride
And seal the title with a lovely kiss.

Exeunt [PETRUCHIO and GRUMIO]

TRANIO
  He hath some meaning in his mad attire.   115
  We will persuade him, be it possible,
  To put on better ere he go to church.

BAPTISTA
  I'll after him, and see the event of this.

Exeunt [BAPTISTA, GREMIO, BIONDELLO, attendants]

TRANIO
  But, sir, to love concerneth us to add
  Her father's liking, which to bring to pass,   120
  As before imparted to your worship,
  I am to get a man—whate'er he be
  It skills not much, we'll fit him to our turn—
  And he shall be Vincentio of Pisa,
  And make assurance here in Padua   125
  Of greater sums than I have promisèd.
  So shall you quietly enjoy your hope
  And marry sweet Bianca with consent.

LUCENTIO
  Were it not that my fellow schoolmaster
  Doth watch Bianca's steps so narrowly,   130
  'Twere good, methinks, to steal our marriage,
  Which once performed, let all the world say no,
   I'll keep mine own despite of all the world.

TRANIO
  That by degrees we mean to look into,
  And watch our vantage in this business.   135
  We'll over-reach the graybeard, Gremio,
  The narrow prying father, Minola,
  The quaint musician, amorous Litio,

148: **fool**: innocent, pitiable person

150: **Should ask**: asked

151: **by gog's wouns**: by God's wounds, an oath

154: **cuff**: strike, beat

156: **list**: wishes, chooses

158–174: **Trembled...play**: set as prose in the First Folio; the Second Folio (1632) sets these lines as verse.

158: **for why**: because

159: **cozen**: trick

All for my master's sake, Lucentio.

Enter GREMIO

Signor Gremio, came you from the church?   140

GREMIO
As willingly as ere I came from school.

TRANIO
And is the bride and bridegroom coming home?

GREMIO
A bridegroom, say you? 'Tis a groom indeed,
A grumbling groom, and that the girl shall find.

TRANIO
Curster than she? Why, 'tis impossible.   145

GREMIO
Why, he's a devil, a devil, a very fiend.

TRANIO
Why she's a devil, a devil, the devil's dam.

GREMIO
Tut, she's a lamb, a dove, a fool to him.
I'll tell you, Sir Lucentio, when the priest
Should ask if Katherine should be his wife,   150
"Ay, by gog's wouns," quoth he, and swore so loud
That all amazed the priest let fall the book,
And as he stooped again to take it up,
This mad-brained bridegroom took him such a cuff
That down fell priest and book, and book and priest.   155
"Now take them up," quoth he, "if any list."

TRANIO
What said the wench when he rose again?

GREMIO
Trembled and shook, for why he stamped and swore
As if the Vicar meant to cozen him.

162: **carousing**: drinking in large quantities

163: **muscatel**: strong, sweet wine

164: **sops**: breads or cakes dipped in water or wine

166: **hungerly**: hungry-looking

172: **rout**: company or crowd of people

173: Stage Direction: ***Music plays***: follows line 174 in the First Folio

174: Stage Direction: ***[GRUMIO and attendants]***: Not in the First Folio; emendation first made by Capell (1768)

175–229: *Roger Allam as Petruchio, Sean Baker as Baptista, Frances Barber as Katherina, and Ensemble*
Petruchio, Baptista, Katherina, and Ensemble from the CBC Radio Adaptations series (1961)

tracks 16-18

182: **Make it no wonder**: do not be amazed at it

But after many ceremonies done,   160
He calls for wine. "A health!" quoth he, as if
He had been aboard carousing to his mates
After a storm, quaffed off the muscatel,
And threw the sops all in the sexton's face,
Having no other reason   165
But that his beard grew thin and hungerly,
And seemed to ask him sops as he was drinking.
This done, he took the bride about the neck
And kissed her lips with such a clamorous smack,
That at the parting all the church did echo.   170
And I, seeing this, came thence for very shame,
And after me I know the rout is coming.
Such a mad marriage never was before.

Music plays

Hark, hark, I hear the minstrels play.
    Enter PETRUCHIO, KATHERINA, BIANCA, HORTENSIO,
              BAPTISTA, [GRUMIO and attendants]

PETRUCHIO
Gentlemen and friends, I thank you for your pains.   175
I know you think to dine with me today,
And have prepared great store of wedding cheer,
But so it is, my haste doth call me hence,
And therefore here I mean to take my leave.

BAPTISTA
Is't possible you will away tonight?   180

PETRUCHIO
I must away today before night come.
Make it no wonder. If you knew my business,
You would entreat me rather go than stay.
And, honest company, I thank you all,
That have beheld me give away myself   185
To this most patient, sweet, and virtuous wife.
Dine with my father, drink a health to me,
For I must hence, and farewell to you all.

tracks 16-18

175–229: *Roger Allam as Petruchio, Sean Baker as Baptista, Frances Barber as Katherina, and Ensemble*
Petruchio, Baptista, Katherina, and Ensemble from the CBC Radio Adaptations series (1961)

Michael Siberry as Petruchio and Josie Lawrence as Katherina in the Royal Shakespeare Company's 1996 production at the Barbican Theatre directed by Gale Edwards
Photo: Donald Cooper

196: the oats...horses: This inversion may simply be a joke, or it may mean that the horses are extremely well fed and therefore ready.

201: jogging...green: proverbial suggestion to hasten the departure of someone unwelcome

TRANIO
Let us entreat you stay till after dinner.

PETRUCHIO
It may not be.

GREMIO
                          Let me entreat you.   190

PETRUCHIO
It cannot be.

KATHERINA
                          Let me entreat you.

PETRUCHIO
I am content.

KATHERINA
                    Are you content to stay?

PETRUCHIO
I am content you shall entreat me stay,
But yet not stay, entreat me how you can.

KATHERINA
Now, if you love me, stay.

PETRUCHIO
                              Grumio, my horse.   195

GRUMIO
Ay, sir, they be ready; the oats have eaten the horses.

KATHERINA
Nay then,
Do what thou canst, I will not go today,
No, nor tomorrow, not till I please myself.
The door is open, sir, there lies your way;   200
You may be jogging whiles your boots are green.

tracks 16-18

175–229: *Roger Allam as Petruchio, Sean Baker as Baptista, Frances Barber as Katherina, and Ensemble*
Petruchio, Baptista, Katherina, and Ensemble from the CBC Radio Adaptations series (1961)

203: **jolly**: 1) self-confident, prideful or 2) (as an intensifier) extremely, very
206: **what...do?**: what business is it of yours?
207: **stay my leisure**: wait until I am ready
214: **domineer**: feast raucously
218: **big**: haughty, defiant

219–223: Scene: **I will be master...whoever dare**: In Taichman's 2007 Shakespeare Theatre Company Production Petruchio (Christopher Innvar) was holding Katherina (Charlayne Woodard) so painfully behind that she was almost crying.

220: **chattels**: goods, movable property
221: **stuff**: goods, movable property
224: **bring mine action**: take legal proceedings against

228: "Fear not, sweet wench, they shall not touch thee, Kate": Jonathan Epstein as Petruchio and Amy van Nostrand as Katherina in the Shakespeare Theatre Company's 1994-1995 production directed by Adrian Hall
Photo: Carol Pratt

229: **buckler**: defend, shield
229: Stage Direction: **Exeunt PETRUCHIO, KATHERINA [and GRUMIO]**: The First Folio reads "*Exeunt. P. Ka*"; Capell (1768) first added Grumio.

For me, I'll not be gone till I please myself.
'Tis like you'll prove a jolly surly groom
That take it on you at the first so roundly.

PETRUCHIO
Oh Kate, content thee, prithee be not angry.   205

KATHERINA
I will be angry; what hast thou to do?
Father, be quiet. He shall stay my leisure.

GREMIO
Ay, marry, sir, now it begins to work.

KATHERINA
Gentlemen, forward to the bridal dinner.
I see a woman may be made a fool   210
If she had not a spirit to resist.

PETRUCHIO
They shall go forward, Kate, at thy command.
Obey the bride, you that attend on her.
Go to the feast, revel and domineer,
Carouse full measure to her maidenhead,   215
Be mad and merry, or go hang yourselves.
But for my bonny Kate, she must with me.
Nay, look not big, nor stamp, nor stare, nor fret;
I will be master of what is mine own.
She is my goods, my chattels; she is my house,   220
My household stuff, my field, my barn,
My horse, my ox, my ass, my anything,
And here she stands. Touch her whoever dare.
I'll bring mine action on the proudest he
That stops my way in Padua. Grumio,   225
Draw forth thy weapon; we are beset with thieves.
Rescue thy mistress if thou be a man.
Fear not, sweet wench, they shall not touch thee, Kate.
I'll buckler thee against a million.
                    Exeunt PETRUCHIO, KATHERINA [and GRUMIO]

Timothy Dalton as Petruchio and Vanessa Redgrave as Katherina in the
Theatre Royal Haymarket's 1986 production directed by Toby Robertson
Photo: Donald Cooper

231: Went they not: if they had not gone

236: wants: are lacking

238: junkets: sweet dishes

240: room: place

241: practice...bride it: play the bride

BAPTISTA
Nay, let them go, a couple of quiet ones.   230

GREMIO
Went they not quickly, I should die with laughing.

TRANIO
Of all mad matches never was the like.

LUCENTIO
Mistress, what's your opinion of your sister?

BIANCA
That being mad herself, she's madly mated.

GREMIO
I warrant him, Petruchio is Kated.   235

BAPTISTA
Neighbors and friends, though bride and bridegroom wants
For to supply the places at the table,
You know there wants no junkets at the feast.
Lucentio, you shall supply the bridegroom's place,
And let Bianca take her sister's room.   240

TRANIO
Shall sweet Bianca practice how to bride it?

BAPTISTA
She shall, Lucentio. Come, gentlemen, let's go.
                                                        Exeunt

[The Taming of
the Shrew

Act 4
z.

0: There is no act or scene division at this point in First Folio (The beginning of Act 4 in the First Folio comes at the beginning of what is now Act 4, scene 3.); Pope first made this division (1723-5).

Set design from the Oregon Shakespeare Festival's 2000 production directed by Kenneth Albers
Set Design: Kent Dorsey: Courtesy of the Oregon Shakespeare Festival

1: **foul ways**: dirty roads

2: **rayed**: dirtied

10: Speech Prefix: **CURTIS**: The First Folio reads "*Gru.*"; this emendation first made in the 1631 quarto.

Act 4, Scene 1]

GRUMIO
Fie, fie on all tired jades, on all mad masters, and all foul ways!
Was ever man so beaten? Was ever man so rayed? Was ever man
so weary? I am sent before to make a fire, and they are coming
after to warm them. Now were not I a little pot and soon hot, my
very lips might freeze to my teeth, my tongue to the roof of my   5
mouth, my heart in my belly, ere I should come by a fire to thaw
me. But I with blowing the fire shall warm myself, for, considering the weather, a taller man than I will take cold. Holla, ho,
Curtis!

Enter CURTIS

CURTIS
Who is that calls so coldly?   10

GRUMIO
A piece of ice. If thou doubt it, thou may'st slide from my
shoulder to my heel, with no greater a run but my head and my
neck. A fire, good Curtis.

CURTIS
Is my master and his wife coming, Grumio?

GRUMIO
Oh, ay, Curtis, ay, and therefore fire, fire, cast on no water.   15

CURTIS
Is she so hot a shrew as she's reported?

GRUMIO
She was, good Curtis, before this frost. But thou know'st winter
tames man, woman and beast, for it hath tamed my old master,
and my new mistress, and myself, fellow Curtis.

20: **three-inch**: i.e., very short

21–22: **Am I...least**: Grumio points out that he may be short, but he is big enough (in more than one sense) to make Curtis a cuckold, i.e., to have sex with Curtis's wife.

22: **on**: about

24: **hot office**: job of providing a fire

30: **"Jack boy, ho boy!"**: a line of a catch, a short song for three or more voices.

31: **cony-catching**: trickery, deception

33: **rushes strewed**: reeds covering the floor

34: **fustian**: coarse cloth made of cotton and flax

36: **Jacks...Jills**: "Jacks" are 1) male servants and 2) leather drinking vessels; "Jills" are 1) female servants and 2) metal drinking vessels.

CURTIS
    Away, you three-inch fool! I am no beast.   20

GRUMIO
    Am I but three inches? Why, thy horn is a foot, and so long am I
    at the least. But wilt thou make a fire, or shall I complain on thee
    to our mistress, whose hand (she being now at hand) thou shalt
    soon feel, to thy cold comfort, for being slow in thy hot office?

CURTIS
    I prithee, good Grumio, tell me, how goes the world?   25

GRUMIO
    A cold world, Curtis, in every office but thine, and therefore fire.
    Do thy duty, and have thy duty, for my master and mistress are
    almost frozen to death.

CURTIS
    There's fire ready, and therefore, good Grumio, the news.

GRUMIO
    Why, "Jack boy, ho boy!" and as much news as wilt thou.   30

CURTIS
    Come, you are so full of cony-catching.

GRUMIO
    Why, therefore fire, for I have caught extreme cold. Where's the
    cook? Is supper ready, the house trimmed, rushes strewed,
    cobwebs swept, the servingmen in their new fustian, the white
    stockings, and every officer his wedding garment on? Be the   35
    Jacks fair within, the Jills fair without, the carpets laid, and
    everything in order?

CURTIS
    All ready, and therefore, I pray thee, news.

GRUMIO
    First, know my horse is tired, my master and mistress fallen out.

45: Stage Direction: *[He strikes him]*: not in the First Folio; this direction was first inserted by Rowe (1709)

48: *Imprimis*: Latin for "first." The First Folio reads "Inprimis", but the Fourth Folio (1685) makes this emendation.

50: **of**: on

CURTIS
    How?   40

GRUMIO
    Out of their saddles into the dirt, and thereby hangs a tale.

CURTIS
    Let's ha't good Grumio.

GRUMIO
    Lend thine ear.

CURTIS
    Here.

GRUMIO
    There.   45
                                                           [He strikes him]

CURTIS
    This 'tis to feel a tale, not to hear a tale.

GRUMIO
    And therefore 'tis called a sensible tale, and this cuff was but to
    knock at your ear, and beseech listening. Now I begin. *Imprimis*
    we came down a foul hill, my master riding behind my mistress.

CURTIS
    Both of one horse?   50

GRUMIO
    What's that to thee?

CURTIS
    Why, a horse.

GRUMIO
    Tell thou the tale. But hadst thou not crossed me, thou shouldst
    have heard how her horse fell, and she under her horse; thou

55: **miry**: boggy, muddy; **bemoiled**: dirty, covered with mud

72: Speech Prefix: **GRUMIO**: The First Folio reads "*Gre.*"; the Third Folio (1663) makes this emendation.

shouldst have heard in how miry a place, how she was bemoiled,   55
how he left her with the horse upon her, how he beat me because
her horse stumbled, how she waded through the dirt to pluck him
off me, how he swore, how she prayed, that never prayed before,
how I cried, how the horses ran away, how her bridle was burst,
how I lost my crupper, with many things of worthy memory,   60
which now shall die in oblivion, and thou return unexperienced to
thy grave.

CURTIS
By this reckoning he is more shrew than she.

GRUMIO
Ay, and that thou and the proudest of you all shall find when he
comes home. But what talk I of this? Call forth Nathaniel,   65
Joseph, Nicholas, Philip, Walter, Sugarsop and the rest; let their
heads be slickly combed, their blue coats brushed, and their
garters of an indifferent knit, let them curtsy with their left legs,
and not presume to touch a hair of my master's horse-tail, till they
kiss their hands. Are they all ready?   70

CURTIS
They are.

GRUMIO
Call them forth.

CURTIS
Do you hear, ho? You must meet my master to countenance my
mistress.

GRUMIO
Why, she hath a face of her own.   75

CURTIS
Who knows not that?

GRUMIO
Thou, it seems, that calls for company to countenance her.

89–90: **Cock's passion**: by God's passion

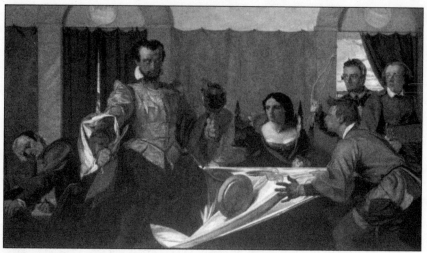

Augustus Egg's painting "Taming of the Shrew" ca. 1860

CURTIS
I call them forth to credit her.

Enter four or five servingmen

GRUMIO
Why, she comes to borrow nothing of them.

NATHANIEL
Welcome home, Grumio.   80

PHILIP
How now, Grumio.

JOSEPH
What, Grumio.

NICHOLAS
Fellow Grumio.

NATHANIEL
How now, old lad.

GRUMIO
Welcome, you; how now, you; what you; fellow you; and thus   85
much for greeting. Now, my spruce companions, is all ready, and
all things neat?

NATHANIEL
All things is ready. How near is our master?

GRUMIO
E'en at hand, alighted by this. And therefore be not—Cock's
passion, silence! I hear my master.   90

Enter PETRUCHIO and KATHERINA

PETRUCHIO
Where be these knaves? What, no man at door
To hold my stirrup, nor to take my horse?
Where is Nathaniel, Gregory, Philip?

96: **logger-headed**: thick-headed, stupid

100: **whoreson**: literally, the son of a whore, but also a common term of derision and contempt; **malt-horse drudge**: belaboured pack animal, meaning heavy and slow

104: **unpinked**: not ornamented (by pinking or piercing with small holes); **i'th'**: in the

105: **link**: blacking made from burnt torches

111: Stage Direction: **[*Sings*]**: not in the First Folio; first inserted by Theobald (1733)

112: **Soud**: perhaps an expression of impatience; some editors have emended this to "food"

Amy van Nostrand as Katherina, Jonathan Epstein as Petruchio, and cast members in the Shakespeare Theatre Company's 1994-1995 production directed by Adrian Hall
Photo: Carol Pratt

115: Stage Direction: **[*Sings*]**: not in the First Folio; first inserted by Rowe (1709). The First Folio prints lines 115–116 in italics.

ALL SERVANTS
    Here, here sir, here sir.

PETRUCHIO
    Here sir, here sir, here sir, here sir!   95
    You logger-headed and unpolished grooms!
    What, no attendance? No regard? No duty?
    Where is the foolish knave I sent before?

GRUMIO
    Here, sir, as foolish as I was before.

PETRUCHIO
    You peasant swain, you whoreson malt-horse drudge!   100
    Did I not bid thee meet me in the park,
    And bring along these rascal knaves with thee?

GRUMIO
    Nathaniel's coat, sir, was not fully made,
    And Gabriel's pumps were all unpinked i' th' heel.
    There was no link to color Peter's hat,   105
    And Walter's dagger was not come from sheathing.
    There were none fine but Adam, Rafe, and Gregory;
    The rest were ragged, old, and beggarly,
    Yet as they are, here are they come to meet you.

PETRUCHIO
    Go, rascals, go, and fetch my supper in.   110
                                Exeunt Servingmen
    [*Sings*]
    Where is the life that late I led?
                        Where are those—
    Sit down, Kate, and welcome. Soud, soud, soud, soud!
                      Enter servants with supper
    Why, when, I say? Nay, good sweet Kate, be merry.
    Off with my boots, you rogues! You villains, when?
    [*Sings*]
    It was the Friar of Orders gray,   115
    As he forth walkèd on his way.

118: Stage Direction: *[Strikes him]*: not in the First Folio; first inserted by Rowe (1709)

121: Stage Direction: *[Exit a servant]*: not in the First Folio; first inserted by Capell (1768)

125: Stage Direction: *[Strikes him]*: not in the First Folio; first inserted by Capell (1768)

127: **beetle-headed**: thick-headed

128: **stomach**: appetite

133: **dresser**: 1) person who dressed or prepared the meat or 2) sideboard or table on which the food has been placed

135: **trenchers**: wooden platters

135: Stage Direction: *[He throws the food and dishes at them]*: not in the First Folio; Rowe (1709) inserts a version of this ("*Throws the Meat, &c. about the Stage*")

Out, you rogue! You pluck my foot awry.
Take that, and mend the plucking of the other.

[Strikes him]

Be merry, Kate. Some water here. What ho!

Enter one with water

Where's my spaniel Troilus? Sirrah, get you hence   120
And bid my cousin Ferdinand come hither.

[Exit a servant]

One, Kate, that you must kiss, and be acquainted with.
Where are my slippers? Shall I have some water?
Come, Kate, and wash, and welcome heartily.
You whoreson villain, will you let it fall?   125

[Strikes him]

KATHERINA
Patience, I pray you, 'twas a fault unwilling.

PETRUCHIO
A whoreson, beetle-headed, flap-eared knave!
Come, Kate, sit down; I know you have a stomach.
Will you give thanks, sweet Kate, or else shall I?
What's this, mutton?

FIRST SERVINGMAN
                Ay.

PETRUCHIO
                Who brought it?

PETER
                                        I.   130

PETRUCHIO
'Tis burnt, and so is all the meat.
What dogs are these? Where is the rascal cook?
How durst you, villains, bring it from the dresser
And serve it thus to me that love it not?
There, take it to you, trenchers, cups, and all.   135

[He throws the food and dishes at them]

136: **joltheads**: blockheads, stupid people

137: Stage Direction: ***[Exeunt Servants]***: not in the First Folio; first inserted by Alexander Dyce (1857)

142: **choler**: irritability of the temper (a reference to the "four humours" of early physiology)

150: **He...humor**: he behaves as she did but is outdoing her

153: **continency**: continence, self-restraint

154: **rates**: berates, scolds

157: Stage Direction: ***[Exeunt]***: not in the First Folio; first inserted by Pope (1723-25)

You heedless joltheads, and unmannered slaves!
What, do you grumble? I'll be with you straight.

[Exeunt Servants]

KATHERINA
I pray you, husband, be not so disquiet.
The meat was well, if you were so contented.

PETRUCHIO
I tell thee, Kate, 'twas burnt and dried away,   140
And I expressly am forbid to touch it,
For it engenders choler, planteth anger;
And better 'twere that both of us did fast,
Since of our selves, our selves are choleric,
Than feed it with such over-roasted flesh.   145
Be patient. Tomorrow't shall be mended,
And for this night we'll fast for company.
Come, I will bring thee to thy bridal chamber.

Exeunt
Enter Servants severally

NATHANIEL
Peter, did'st ever see the like?

PETER
He kills her in her own humor.   150

GRUMIO
Where is he?

Enter CURTIS

CURTIS
In her chamber,
Making a sermon of continency to her,
And rails, and swears, and rates, that she (poor soul)
Knows not which way to stand, to look, to speak,   155
And sits as one new-risen from a dream.
Away, away, for he is coming hither.

[Exeunt]
Enter PETRUCHIO

158: **politicly**: shrewdly, prudently

158–181: Scene: **Thus have. . .to shew**: John Cleese, in Miller's 1980 BBC film, sounded weary, worried and thoughtful. In Doran's 2003 RSC production Petruchio (Jasper Britton) said the first two lines defiantly then went on uncertainly. In Bill Alexander's 1992 RSC production Petruchio (Anton Lesser) gave his speech in the presence of and partly to two of the servants, not as a soliloquy. He sounded very worried. In Jude Kelly's 1993 West Yorkshire Playhouse production Katherina overheard the speech and Petruchio looked up and saw that she had.

160: **My falcon now is sharp**: hungry

161: **stoop**: (of a hawk or bird of prey, or with reference to the lure in falconry) descend swiftly, swoop; **full gorged**: allowed to eat her fill

162: **lure**: (in falconry) apparatus used to call and feed the hawk generally consisting of a bunch of feathers attached to a cord meant to imitate a bird in motion

163: **man my haggard**: tame my wild hawk

165: **kites**: falcons

166: **bait, and beat**: flutter and flap their wings

173: **hurly**: uproar, commotion; **intend**: pretend, claim

PETRUCHIO
   Thus have I politicly begun my reign,
   And 'tis my hope to end successfully.
   My falcon now is sharp and passing empty,   160
   And till she stoop, she must not be full gorged,
   For then she never looks upon her lure.
   Another way I have to man my haggard,
   To make her come, and know her keeper's call.
   That is, to watch her, as we watch these kites   165
   That bait, and beat, and will not be obedient.
   She ate no meat today, nor none shall eat.
   Last night she slept not, nor tonight she shall not.
   As with the meat, some undeservèd fault
   I'll find about the making of the bed,   170
   And here I'll fling the pillow, there the bolster,
   This way the coverlet, another way the sheets.
   Ay, and amid this hurly I intend
   That all is done in reverend care of her.
   And in conclusion, she shall watch all night,   175
   And if she chance to nod, I'll rail and brawl,
   And with the clamor keep her still awake.
   This is a way to kill a wife with kindness,
   And thus I'll curb her mad and headstrong humor.
   He that knows better how to tame a shrew,   180
   Now let him speak; 'tis charity to shew.

                             Exit

0: no scene division in First Folio; George Steevens first made this division in 1778.

3: **bears...hand**: leads me on or deceives me beautifully

4: Speech Prefix: **HORTENSIO**: The First Folio reads "*Luc.*" despite the opening stage direction; the Second Folio (1632) corrects this error.

5: Stage Direction: *[They stand aside.]*: not in the First Folio; first inserted (as "*They stand by*") by Theobald (1733)

5: Stage Direction: *[and LUCENTIO]*: not in the First Folio; first inserted by Rowe (1709)

6: Speech Prefix: **LUCENTIO**: The First Folio reads "*Hor.*"; the Second Folio (1632) made this correction.

8: ***The Art to Love***: Ovid's *Ars Amatoria* (see note 1.1.33)

11: **proceeders**: scholars or students

13: **none**: The First Folio reads "me"; Rowe first made this emendation (1709).

Set design from the Oregon Shakespeare Festival's 2000 production directed by Kenneth Albers
Set Design: Kent Dorsey. Courtesy of the Oregon Shakespeare Festival

14: **despiteful**: cruel

15: **wonderful**: astonishing

Act 4, Scene 2]

TRANIO
    Is't possible, friend Litio, that mistress Bianca
    Doth fancy any other but Lucentio?
    I tell you, sir, she bears me fair in hand.

HORTENSIO
    Sir, to satisfy you in what I have said,
    Stand by, and mark the manner of his teaching.   5
                [They stand aside.] Enter BIANCA [and LUCENTIO].

LUCENTIO
Now, mistress, profit you in what you read?

BIANCA
    What, master, read you? First resolve me that.

HORTENSIO
    I read that I profess, *The Art to Love*.

BIANCA
    And may you prove, sir, master of your art.

LUCENTIO
    While you, sweet dear, prove mistress of my heart.   10

HORTENSIO
    Quick proceeders, marry! Now tell me, I pray,
    You that durst swear that your mistress Bianca
    Loved none in the world so well as Lucentio.

TRANIO
    Oh despiteful love, unconstant womankind!
    I tell thee, Litio, this is wonderful.   15

20: **cullion**: despicable fellow or base rascal

24: **lightness**: wantonness

31: **fondly**: foolishly; **her**: The First Folio reads "them"; the Third Folio (1663) makes this emendation.

34: **beastly**: like an animal

39: **haggard**: wild female hawk

43: Stage Direction: *[Exit]*: not in the First Folio; first inserted by Rowe (1709)

HORTENSIO

    Mistake no more. I am not Litio,
    Nor a musician as I seem to be,
    But one that scorn to live in this disguise
    For such a one as leaves a gentleman
    And makes a god of such a cullion.   20
    Know, sir, that I am called Hortensio.

TRANIO

    Signor Hortensio, I have often heard
    Of your entire affection to Bianca,
    And since mine eyes are witness of her lightness,
    I will with you, if you be so contented,   25
    Forswear Bianca and her love forever.

HORTENSIO

    See how they kiss and court! Signor Lucentio,
    Here is my hand, and here I firmly vow
    Never to woo her more, but do forswear her
    As one unworthy all the former favors   30
    That I have fondly flattered her withal.

TRANIO

    And here I take the like unfeignèd oath
    Never to marry with her, though she would entreat.
    Fie on her! See how beastly she doth court him.

HORTENSIO

    Would all the world but he had quite forsworn   35
    For me, that I may surely keep mine oath,
    I will be married to a wealthy widow,
    Ere three days pass, which hath as long loved me
    As I have loved this proud disdainful haggard.
    And so farewell, Signor Lucentio,   40
    Kindness in women, not their beauteous looks,
    Shall win my love, and so I take my leave,
    In resolution as I swore before.

                                                             [Exit]

45: **'longeth**: belongs

46: **ta'en you**: caught you

57: **tricks eleven and twenty long**: just the right tricks

58: **charm...tongue**: silence her by magic

TRANIO

    Mistress Bianca, bless you with such grace

    As 'longeth to a lover's blessed case.   45

    Nay, I have ta'en you napping, gentle love,

    And have forsworn you with Hortensio.

BIANCA

    Tranio, you jest, but have you both forsworn me?

TRANIO

    Mistress, we have.

LUCENTIO

               Then we are rid of Litio.

TRANIO

    I' faith he'll have a lusty widow now   50

    That shall be wooed and wedded in a day.

BIANCA

    God give him joy!

TRANIO

    Ay, and he'll tame her.

BIANCA

               He says so, Tranio.

TRANIO

    Faith he is gone unto the taming-school.

BIANCA

    The taming-school? What, is there such a place?   55

TRANIO

    Ay, mistress, and Petruchio is the master,

    That teacheth tricks eleven and twenty long,

    To tame a shrew, and charm her chattering tongue.

                                Enter BIONDELLO

61: **ancient angel**: fellow of the good old stamp ("the angel" was an old English coin with the figure of the archangel Michael)

62: **serve the turn**: suit our purpose

63: **marcantant**: merchant (a version of the Italian *mercatante*)

70–71: **As if...Vincentio. / Take in...alone**: The First Folio has a speech prefix "Par." between these two lines; it was removed in the Second Folio (1632). (W. W. Greg speculated in 1955 that this might be the name of the actor due to speak as Pedant in line 72)

71: **in**: The First Folio reads "me"; Lewis Theobald (1733) first made this emendation.

71: Stage Direction: *[Exeunt LUCENTIO and BIANCA]*: not in the First Folio; first inserted by Rowe (1709)

73: **far on**: farther

BIONDELLO
  Oh master, master, I have watched so long
  That I am dog-weary, but at last I spied   60
  An ancient angel coming down the hill
  Will serve the turn.

TRANIO
                    What is he Biondello?

BIONDELLO
  Master, a marcantant, or a pedant,
  I know not what, but formal in apparel,
  In gait and countenance surely like a father.   65

LUCENTIO
  And what of him, Tranio?

TRANIO
  If he be credulous and trust my tale
  I'll make him glad to seem Vincentio,
  And give assurance to Baptista Minola,
  As if he were the right Vincentio.   70
  Take in your love, and then let me alone.
                          [Exeunt LUCENTIO and BIANCA]
                                    Enter a PEDANT

PEDANT
  God save you, sir.

TRANIO
                    And you sir, you are welcome,
  Travel you far on, or are you at the farthest?

PEDANT
  Sir, at the farthest for a week or two,
  But then up farther, and as far as Rome,   75
  And so to Tripoli, if God lend me life.

80: **that goes hard**: that is serious

83: **stayed**: detained

89: **bills for money by exchange**: written orders or promissory notes to be exchanged for cash.

95: **Pisa...citizens**: an identical line occurs at 1.1.10

TRANIO
    What countryman I pray?

PEDANT

                    Of Mantua.

TRANIO
    Of Mantua, Sir? Marry, God forbid!
    And come to Padua, careless of your life?

PEDANT
    My life, sir? How, I pray? For that goes hard.   80

TRANIO
    'Tis death for any one in Mantua
    To come to Padua. Know you not the cause?
    Your ships are stayed at Venice, and the Duke
    For private quarrel 'twixt your Duke and him,
    Hath published and proclaimed it openly.   85
    'Tis marvel, but that you are but newly come,
    You might have heard it else proclaimed about.

PEDANT
    Alas, sir, it is worse for me than so,
    For I have bills for money by exchange
    From Florence, and must here deliver them.   90

TRANIO
    Well, sir, to do you courtesy,
    This will I do, and this I will advise you.
    First tell me, have you ever been at Pisa?

PEDANT
    Ay, sir, in Pisa have I often been,
    Pisa renownèd for grave citizens.   95

TRANIO
    Among them know you one Vincentio?

101: Stage Direction: *[Aside]*: not in the First Folio; emendation first made by Rowe (1709)

101: **As much...oyster**: proverbial

106: **credit**: reputation; **undertake**: assume, take on

108: **take upon you**: do what is required of you

112: **repute**: consider

114: **make the matter good**: carry out the plan

116: **looked for**: expected

117: **pass assurance of**: make a legal agreement

PEDANT
    I know him not, but I have heard of him:
    A merchant of incomparable wealth.

TRANIO
    He is my father, sir, and sooth to say,
    In count'nance somewhat doth resemble you.   100

BIONDELLO
    [*Aside*] As much as an apple doth an oyster, and all one.

TRANIO
    To save your life in this extremity,
    This favor will I do you for his sake,
    And think it not the worst of all your fortunes.
    That you are like to Sir Vincentio.   105
    His name and credit shall you undertake,
    And in my house you shall be friendly lodged.
    Look that you take upon you as you should.
    You understand me, sir. So shall you stay
    Till you have done your business in the city.   110
    If this be court'sy, sir, accept of it.

PEDANT
    Oh sir, I do, and will repute you ever
    The patron of my life and liberty.

TRANIO
    Then go with me, to make the matter good.
    This, by the way, I let you understand: 115
    My father is here looked for every day,
    To pass assurance of a dower in marriage
    'Twixt me, and one Baptista's daughter here.
    In all these circumstances I'll instruct you.
    Go with me to clothe you as becomes you.   120
                                         Exeunt

0: The First Folio reads "*Actus Quartus. Scena Prima*"; George Steevens first made this division in 1773.

tracks 19-21

1-35:
Katherina and Grumio from the CBC Radio Adaptations series (1961)
Frances Barber as Katherina and Michael Higgs as Grumio

2: **The more my wrong**: the greater the wrong done to me
5: **present**: immediate
9: **meat**: food
11: **spites**: annoys
13: **As...say**: as if to say, or like one who says
16: **so it be**: as long as it is
17: **neat's**: ox's or cow's

19: "I fear it is too choleric a meat": Joel Brooks as Grumio and Meryl Streep as Katherine in the 1977-78 Public Theatre production directed by Wilford Leach
Photo: George E. Joseph

20: **tripe**: stomach of a ruminant (e.g., an ox) prepared as food

Act 4, Scene 3]

GRUMIO
No, no, forsooth, I dare not for my life.

KATHERINA
The more my wrong, the more his spite appears.
What, did he marry me to famish me?
Beggars that come unto my father's door
Upon entreaty have a present alms;   5
If not, elsewhere they meet with charity.
But I, who never knew how to entreat,
Nor never needed that I should entreat,
Am starved for meat, giddy for lack of sleep,
With oaths kept waking, and with brawling fed.   10
And that which spites me more than all these wants,
He does it under name of perfect love,
As who should say, if I should sleep or eat
'Twere deadly sickness, or else present death.
I prithee go and get me some repast,   15
I care not what, so it be wholesome food.

GRUMIO
What say you to a neat's foot?

KATHERINA
'Tis passing good; I prithee let me have it.

GRUMIO
I fear it is too choleric a meat.
How say you to a fat tripe finely broiled?   20

KATHERINA
I like it well; good Grumio, fetch it me.

tracks 19-21

1-35:
Katherina and Grumio from the CBC Radio Adaptations series (1961)
Frances Barber as Katherina and Michael Higgs as Grumio

Amy van Nostrand as Katherina in the Shakespeare Theatre
Company's 1994-1995 production directed by Adrian Hall
Photo: Carol Pratt

32: **the very name:** just the name

36: **sweeting:** dear one, darling; **all amort:** dejected, dispirited

GRUMIO
    I cannot tell; I fear 'tis choleric.
    What say you to a piece of beef and mustard?

KATHERINA
    A dish that I do love to feed upon.

GRUMIO
    Ay, but the mustard is too hot a little.   25

KATHERINA
    Why then the beef, and let the mustard rest.

GRUMIO
    Nay then, I will not; you shall have the mustard
    Or else you get no beef of Grumio.

KATHERINA
    Then both or one, or anything thou wilt.

GRUMIO
    Why then the mustard without the beef.   30

KATHERINA
    Go, get thee gone, thou false deluding slave,

                                        Beats him

    That feed'st me with the very name of meat.
    Sorrow on thee, and all the pack of you
    That triumph thus upon my misery.
    Go, get thee gone, I say.   35
              Enter PETRUCHIO and HORTENSIO with meat

PETRUCHIO
    How fares my Kate? What, sweeting, all amort?

HORTENSIO
    Mistress, what cheer?

KATHERINA
               Faith, as cold as can be.

43: **And all...proof**: all my effort has been in vain

50: Stage Direction: ***[Aside]***: not in the First Folio; first inserted by Theobald (1733)

54: **bravely**: dressed finely, handsomely

56: **ruffs**: starched, fluted neckwear; **farthingales**: hooped petticoats

57: **brav'ry**: finery

58: **this knav'ry**: these tricks, this nonsense

59: **stays**: awaits

60: **ruffling**: ruffled

62: Stage Direction: ***Enter HABERDASHER***: follows line 61 in the First Folio; emendation first made by Alexander Dyce (1857)

PETRUCHIO
    Pluck up thy spirits; look cheerfully upon me.
    Here, love, thou seest how diligent I am,
    To dress thy meat myself, and bring it thee.   40
    I am sure, sweet Kate, this kindness merits thanks.
    What, not a word? Nay then, thou lov'st it not,
    And all my pains is sorted to no proof.
    Here, take away this dish.

KATHERINA
                    I pray you let it stand.

PETRUCHIO
    The poorest service is repaid with thanks,   45
    And so shall mine before you touch the meat.

KATHERINA
    I thank you, sir.

HORTENSIO
    Signor Petruchio, fie, you are to blame.
    Come, Mistress Kate, I'll bear you company.

PETRUCHIO
    [*Aside*] Eat it up all, Hortensio, if thou lovest me.—   50
    Much good do it unto thy gentle heart.
    Kate, eat apace. And now, my honey love,
    Will we return unto thy father's house,
    And revel it as bravely as the best,
    With silken coats and caps, and golden rings,   55
    With ruffs and cuffs and farthingales and things,
    With scarves and fans and double change of brav'ry,
    With amber bracelets, beads, and all this knav'ry.
    What, hast thou dined? The tailor stays thy leisure,
    To deck thy body with his ruffling treasure.   60
                            Enter TAILOR

    Come, Tailor, let us see these ornaments.
    Lay forth the gown.
                       Enter HABERDASHER
            What news with you, sir?

63: Speech Prefix: **HABERDASHER**: the First Folio reads "*Fel.*"; emendation first made by Rowe (1709)

64: **porringer**: small bowl or basin

65: **lewd and filthy**: G. R. Hibbard (1968) describes this as the Elizabethan equivalent of "cheap and nasty."

66: **cockle**: cockleshell

67: **knack**: trifle, knick-knack

69: **doth fit the time**: is fashionable

69-70: "I'll have no bigger; this doth fit the time, / And gentlewomen wear such caps as these": Norris M. Shimabuku as Tailor, Morgan Freeman as Petruchio, and Tracey Ullman as Katherina in the 1989-90 Public Theatre production directed by A. J. Antoon
Photo: George E. Joseph

75: **endured me**: let me

81: **is a paltry**: The First Folio reads "is paltry"; this emendation was first made in 1631

82: **custard coffin**: pastry crust for a custard

85: Stage Direction: *[Exit HABERDASHER]*: not in the First Folio; emendation first made in the 1863–6 Cambridge edition

HABERDASHER
    Here is the cap your worship did bespeak.

PETRUCHIO
    Why this was molded on a porringer—
    A velvet dish. Fie, fie, 'tis lewd and filthy,   65
    Why 'tis a cockle or a walnut-shell,
    A knack, a toy, a trick, a baby's cap.
    Away with it! Come, let me have a bigger.

KATHERINA
    I'll have no bigger; this doth fit the time,
    And gentlewomen wear such caps as these.   70

PETRUCHIO
    When you are gentle, you shall have one too,
    And not till then.

HORTENSIO
                        That will not be in haste.

KATHERINA
    Why, sir, I trust I may have leave to speak,
    And speak I will. I am no child, no babe.
    Your betters have endured me say my mind,   75
    And if you cannot, best you stop your ears.
    My tongue will tell the anger of my heart,
    Or else my heart concealing it will break,
    And rather than it shall, I will be free
    Even to the uttermost, as I please, in words.   80

PETRUCHIO
    Why, thou say'st true; it is a paltry cap,
    A custard coffin, a bauble, a silken pie.
    I love thee well in that thou lik'st it not.

KATHERINA
    Love me, or love me not, I like the cap,
    And it I will have, or I will have none.   85
                                    [Exit HABERDASHER]

Elizabeth Taylor as Kate in the 1967 film directed by Franco Zeffirelli
Copyright © 1966 Columbia Pictures, Courtesy of Douglas Lanier

87: **masking stuff**: clothing suitable for a masque but not for normal wear
88: **like a demi-**: the First Folio reads "like demi"; emendation first made in the 1631 quarto; **demi-cannon**: large cannon
91: **censor**: incense-burner
93: Stage Direction: **[*Aside*]**: not in the First Folio; first inserted by Theobald (1733)
97: **mar**: spoil
98: **kennel**: gutter
106: **Oh...thimble**: appears as two lines in the First Folio, divided between "arrogance!" and " Thou".
107: **nail**: sixteenth of a yard
108: **nit**: egg of a louse
109: **Braved**: challenged, defied

PETRUCHIO
    Thy gown? Why, ay. Come, Tailor, let us see't.
    Oh mercy God, what masking stuff is here?
    What's this? A sleeve? 'Tis like a demi-cannon.
    What, up and down carved like an apple tart?
    Here's snip and nip and cut and slish and slash,   90
    Like to a censor in a barber's shop.
    Why what a devil's name, tailor, call'st thou this?

HORTENSIO
    [*Aside*] I see she's like to have neither cap nor gown.

TAILOR
    You bid me make it orderly and well,
    According to the fashion and the time.   95

PETRUCHIO
    Marry and did. But if you be remembered,
    I did not bid you mar it to the time.
    Go, hop me over every kennel home,
    For you shall hop without my custom, sir.
    I'll none of it; hence, make your best of it.   100

KATHERINA
    I never saw a better fashioned gown,
    More quaint, more pleasing, nor more commendable.
    Belike you mean to make a puppet of me.

PETRUCHIO
    Why, true, he means to make a puppet of thee.

TAILOR
    She says your worship means to make a puppet of her.   105

PETRUCHIO
    Oh monstrous arrogance! Thou liest, thou thread, thou thimble,
    Thou yard, three quarters, half yard, quarter, nail!
    Thou flea, thou nit, thou winter cricket thou!
    Braved in mine own house with a skein of thread?

111: **bemete**: measure; **yard**: yardstick

112: **As thou shalt think on prating**: so that you will think before chattering

117: **stuff**: material

117–126: Scene: **I gave...thou liest**: In Doran's 2003 RSC Katherina (Alexandra Gilbreath) sat on the floor gripping the remnants of her wrecked dress, at first looking up at Petruchio (Jasper Britton) and then apparently mourning over the ruins of the dress. By the end of the scene Katherina was weeping as Petruchio delivered his speech (163–182) about the unimportance of dress.

121: **faced**: 1) trimmed also 2) confronted or bullied

125: *Ergo*: therefore

Away, thou rag, thou quantity, thou remnant,   110
Or I shall so bemete thee with thy yard
As thou shalt think on prating whil'st thou liv'st:
I tell thee, I, that thou hast marred her gown.

TAILOR
Your worship is deceived; the gown is made
Just as my master had direction.   115
Grumio gave order how it should be done.

GRUMIO
I gave him no order; I gave him the stuff.

TAILOR
But how did you desire it should be made?

GRUMIO
Marry, sir, with needle and thread.

TAILOR
But did you not request to have it cut?   120

GRUMIO
Thou hast faced many things.

TAILOR
I have.

GRUMIO
Face not me. Thou hast braved many men; brave not me. I will
neither be faced nor braved. I say unto thee, I bid thy master cut
out the gown, but I did not bid him cut it to pieces. *Ergo,* thou   125
liest.

TAILOR
Why, here is the note of the fashion to testify.

PETRUCHIO
Read it.

129: **in's**: in his; **lies in's throat**: tells a flat-out lie

130: *Imprimis*: the First Folio reads "Inprimis"; the Third Folio (1663) makes this emendation.

132: **bottom**: skein or ball

135: **compassed**: cut in a circular shape

137: **trunk sleeve**: full sleeve

142–143: **prove upon thee**: prove in single combat

144: **and I...where**: if I had you in a suitable place

GRUMIO
The note lies in's throat if he say I said so.

TAILOR
Imprimis, a loose-bodied gown.   130

GRUMIO
Master, if ever I said "loose-bodied gown," sew me in the skirts of
it, and beat me to death with a bottom of brown thread: I said a
gown.

PETRUCHIO
Proceed.

TAILOR
With a small-compassed cape.   135

GRUMIO
I confess the cape.

TAILOR
With a trunk sleeve.

GRUMIO
I confess two sleeves.

TAILOR
The sleeves curiously cut.

PETRUCHIO
Ay, there's the villainy.   140

GRUMIO
Error i' th' bill, sir, error i' th' bill? I commanded the sleeves
should be cut out, and sewed up again, and that I'll prove upon
thee, though thy little finger be armed in a thimble.

TAILOR
This is true that I say, and I had thee in place where, thou
should'st know it.   145

146: **for thee straight**: ready for you straight away; **mete-yard**: measuring rod

148: **odds**: advantage

151: **take...use**: take it away and let your master make of it whatever use he chooses

154: **conceit**: idea

158: Stage Direction: *[Aside]*: not in the First Folio; first inserted by Rowe (1709)

160: Stage Direction: *[Aside]*: not in the First Folio; first inserted by Capell (1768)

GRUMIO
    I am for thee straight. Take thou the bill, give me thy mete-yard,
    and spare not me.

HORTENSIO
    God-a-mercy, Grumio, then he shall have no odds.

PETRUCHIO
    Well, sir, in brief, the gown is not for me.

GRUMIO
    You are i' th' right, sir, 'tis for my mistress.   150

PETRUCHIO
    Go, take it up unto thy master's use.

GRUMIO
    Villain, not for thy life! Take up my mistress' gown for thy
    master's use!

PETRUCHIO
    Why, sir, what's your conceit in that?

GRUMIO
    Oh, sir, the conceit is deeper than you think for.   155
    Take up my mistress' gown to his master's use?
    Oh fie, fie, fie!

PETRUCHIO
    [*Aside*] Hortensio, say thou wilt see the tailor paid.—
    Go, take it hence, be gone, and say no more.

HORTENSIO
    [*Aside*] Tailor, I'll pay thee for thy gown tomorrow.   160
    Take no unkindness of his hasty words.
    Away, I say; commend me to thy master.

                                            Exit TAILOR

164: **honest mean habiliments**: respectable, humble clothes

168: **peereth in**: can be seen peeping through

174: **furniture**: outfit

175: **account'st**: the First Folio reads "accountedst"; emendation first made by Rowe (1709)

177: **sport us**: enjoy ourselves

Meryl Streep as Katherine in the 1977-78 Public Theatre
production directed by Wilford Leach
Photo: George E. Joseph

182: **dinner time**: about noon

186: **Look what**: whatever

187: **still crossing**: always contradicting

185-189: Scene: **It shall...it is**: Fiona Shaw (Katherina in Miller's 1987 RSC production) has commented: "God, what a line! Shakespeare is sailing so close to the wind...I think Petruchio is playing another of those word games that haven't yet quite clicked with Kate. Understandably, she is blind to the freeing possibilities of conceding anything, having becomes a barnacled custodian of reaction" (*Clamorous Voices*).

190: Stage Direction: **[Aside]**: not in the First Folio; first inserted by Irving (1888-90)

190: Stage Direction: **[Exeunt]** : not in the First Folio; first inserted by Rowe (1709)

PETRUCHIO
    Well, come, my Kate, we will unto your father's,
    Even in these honest mean habiliments.
    Our purses shall be proud, our garments poor,   165
    For 'tis the mind that makes the body rich.
    And as the sun breaks through the darkest clouds,
    So honor peereth in the meanest habit.
    What, is the jay more precious than the lark
    Because his feathers are more beautiful?   170
    Or is the adder better than the eel
    Because his painted skin contents the eye?
    Oh no, good Kate; neither art thou the worse
    For this poor furniture, and mean array.
    If thou account'st it shame, lay it on me,   175
    And therefore frolic. We will hence forthwith,
    To feast and sport us at thy father's house.
    Go call my men, and let us straight to him,
    And bring our horses unto Long-lane end.
    There will we mount, and thither walk on foot,   180
    Let's see, I think 'tis now some seven o'clock,
    And well we may come there by dinner time.

KATHERINA
    I dare assure you, sir, 'tis almost two,
    And 'twill be supper-time ere you come there.

PETRUCHIO
    It shall be seven ere I go to horse.   185
    Look what I speak, or do, or think to do,
    You are still crossing it. Sirs, let't alone.
    I will not go to day, and ere I do,
    It shall be what o'clock I say it is.

HORTENSIO
    [*Aside*] Why so this gallant will command the sun.   190
                                  [Exeunt]

0: no scene division in the First Folio; George Steevens first made this division in 1773.

0: Stage Direction: *[booted and bareheaded]*: In First Folio this additional description appears wrongly in the stage direction at line 18.

1: **Sir**: The First Folio reads "Sirs"; Lewis Theobald (1733) first made this emendation

2: **but**: unless

5: **Where...Pegasus**: The First Folio, assigned this line to Tranio in the First Folio and was re-assigned to Pedant by Lewis Theobald (1733). The Pegasus, from the mythological winged horse, is an inn; in Shakespeare's time it was a popular inn sign.

8: Stage Direction: *Enter BIONDELLO*: In the First Folio, the stage direction follows line 7; in the 1928 New Cambridge edition (Sir Arthur Quiller-Couch and John Dover Wilson) it appears in line 8 (as Biondello approaches).

9: **schooled**: trained in his part

11: **throughly**: thoroughly

Act 4, Scene 4]

Enter TRANIO, and the PEDANT dressed like Vincentio,
[booted and bareheaded]

TRANIO
Sir, this is the house. Please it you that I call?

PEDANT
Ay, what else, and but I be deceived,
Signor Baptista may remember me
Near twenty years ago in Genoa
Where we were lodgers at the Pegasus.   5

TRANIO
'Tis well, and hold your own in any case
With such austerity as 'longeth to a father.

PEDANT
I warrant you.

Enter BIONDELLO

              But, sir, here comes your boy,
'Twere good he were schooled.

TRANIO
Fear you not him. Sirrah Biondello,   10
Now do your duty throughly, I advise you:
Imagine 'twere the right Vincentio.

BIONDELLO
Tut, fear not me.

TRANIO
But hast thou done thy errand to Baptista?

BIONDELLO
I told him that your father was at Venice,   15
And that you looked for him this day in Padua.

17: **tall**: fine, skilful; **hold...drink**: use that to buy yourself a drink

18: Stage Direction: ***Enter BAPTISTA and LUCENTIO***: The First Folio reads *"Enter Baptista and Lucentio: Pedant booted and bare headed"*; Pope (1723-5) removed the last five words.

26: **weighty cause**: important matter

28: **for**: because of

30: **stay**: delay

32: **like**: approve

36: **curious**: over-particular, fussy

42: Scene: **Or...affections**: In Doran's 2003 RSC production Baptista (Ian Gelder) said this as a great piece of wit and it was treated with awkward, exaggerated hilarity by his listeners.

45: **pass**: settle on, grant to

TRANIO
> Th'art a tall fellow; hold thee that to drink.
> Here comes Baptista. Set your countenance sir.
>> *Enter BAPTISTA and LUCENTIO*

TRANIO
> Signor Baptista you are happily met.
> Sir, this is the gentleman I told you of.   20
> I pray you stand good father to me now;
> Give me Bianca for my patrimony.

PEDANT
> Soft, son.
> Sir, by your leave, having come to Padua
> To gather in some debts, my son Lucentio   25
> Made me acquainted with a weighty cause
> Of love between your daughter and himself.
> And, for the good report I hear of you,
> And for the love he beareth to your daughter,
> And she to him, to stay him not too long,   30
> I am content in a good father's care
> To have him matched; and if you please to like
> No worse than I, upon some agreement
> Me shall you find ready and willing
> With one consent to have her so bestowed,   35
> For curious I cannot be with you,
> Signor Baptista, of whom I hear so well.

BAPTISTA
> Sir, pardon me in what I have to say.
> Your plainness and your shortness please me well.
> Right true it is your son Lucentio here   40
> Doth love my daughter, and she loveth him,
> Or both dissemble deeply their affections.
> And therefore, if you say no more than this,
> That like a father you will deal with him,
> And pass my daughter a sufficient dower,   45
> The match is made, and all is done.
> Your son shall have my daughter with consent.

49: **affied**: affianced, formally betrothed

52: **Pitchers have ears**: proverbial, implying that others might be listening or eavesdropping

53: **heark'ning**: listening

54: **happily**: by chance, perhaps

55: **and it like**: if it please

56: **lie**: lodge, stay

59: **scrivener**: notary

60: **slender**: slight, brief

61: **pittance**: meagre meal

62: **hie you**: go quickly

62–63: **It likes...ready straight**: In the First Folio, the line ends after "well" and the next (long) line begins with "Cambio"; George Steevens first made this division in 1773.

68–69: Stage Direction: The First Folio has *"Enter Peter"* between these lines, but this appears to be a mistake.

68: Stage Direction: ***Exit [BIONDELLO]***: The stage direction (without a name) follows line 67 in the First Folio.

70: **mess**: dish or course; **cheer**: entertainment or hospitality

TRANIO

    I thank you, sir. Where then do you know best
    We be affied and such assurance ta'en
    As shall with either part's agreement stand?   50

BAPTISTA

    Not in my house, Lucentio, for you know
    Pitchers have ears, and I have many servants;
    Besides, old Gremio is heark'ning still,
    And happily we might be interrupted.

TRANIO

    Then at my lodging, and it like you.   55
    There doth my father lie, and there this night
    We'll pass the business privately and well.
    Send for your daughter by your servant here;
    My boy shall fetch the scrivener presently,
    The worst is this, that at so slender warning,   60
    You are like to have a thin and slender pittance.

BAPTISTA

    It likes me well. Cambio, hie you home,
    And bid Bianca make her ready straight.
    And if you will, tell what hath happenèd:
    Lucentio's father is arrived in Padua,   65
    And how she's like to be Lucentio's wife.

                         [Exit LUCENTIO]

BIONDELLO

    I pray the gods she may with all my heart.

TRANIO

    Dally not with the gods, but get thee gone.

                         Exit [BIONDELLO]

    Signor Baptista, shall I lead the way?
    Welcome. One mess is like to be your cheer.   70
    Come, sir, we will better it in Pisa.

77: **'has**: he has. The First Folio reads "has"; Thomas Hanmer (1744) first made this emendation (to "ha's").

79: **moralize**: explain, interpret

BAPTISTA
I follow you.

Exeunt
Enter LUCENTIO and BIONDELLO

BIONDELLO
Cambio!

LUCENTIO
What say'st thou, Biondello?

BIONDELLO
You saw my master wink and laugh upon you?   75

LUCENTIO
Biondello, what of that?

BIONDELLO
Faith, nothing; but 'has left me here behind to expound the meaning or moral of his signs and tokens.

LUCENTIO
I pray thee, moralize them.

BIONDELLO
Then thus: Baptista is safe, talking with the deceiving father of a   80
deceitful son.

LUCENTIO
And what of him?

BIONDELLO
His daughter is to be brought by you to the supper.

LUCENTIO
And then?

BIONDELLO
The old priest at Saint Luke's Church is at your command at all   85
hours.

88: **except**: The First Folio reads "expect"; the Second Folio (1632) makes this emendation.

89: **assurance**: legal settlement

89–90: *cum...solum*: with the exclusive right to print; this formula appeared on the title-page of many books, sometimes abbreviated to *cum privilegio*. The First Folio reads "*Cum previlegio ad Impremendum solem,*" which was corrected in the Second Folio (1632).

95: **tarry**: delay, linger

98: **against you come**: in preparation for your coming

99: **appendix**: appendage (i.e., the bride); also a continuation of Biondello's printing joke

102: **Hap what hap may, I'll roundly go about her**: no matter what happens, I will tackle her directly.

LUCENTIO
And what of all this?

BIONDELLO
I cannot tell, except they are busied about a counterfeit assurance.
Take you assurance of her, *cum privilegio ad imprimendum
solum*, to th' church take the priest, clerk, and some sufficient   90
honest witnesses.
  If this be not that you look for, I have no more to say,
  But bid Bianca farewell for ever and a day.

LUCENTIO
Hear'st thou, Biondello?

BIONDELLO
I cannot tarry. I knew a wench married in an afternoon as she   95
went to the garden for parsley to stuff a rabbit, and so may you,
sir. And so adieu, sir; my master hath appointed me to go to Saint
Luke's to bid the priest be ready to come against you come with
your appendix.

                                                                  Exit

LUCENTIO
I may and will, if she be so contented.   100
She will be pleased, then wherefore should I doubt?
Hap what hap may, I'll roundly go about her.
It shall go hard if Cambio go without her.

                                                                  Exit

0: no scene division in the First Folio; George Steevens made this division in 1773

0: Stage Direction: *[and Servants]*: not in the First Folio; emendation first made by Clark and Glover in the 1863-6 Cambridge edition.

5: "I know it is the sun that shines so bright": Sinead Cusack as Katherina, Ian Talbot as Hortensio, Pete Postlethwaite as Grumio, and Alun Armstron as Petruchio in the Royal Shakespeare Company's 1983 production directed by Barry Kyle
Photo: Donald Cooper

tracks 22-24

2-48:
Roger Allam as Petruchio and Frances Barber as Katherina
Marc Singer as Petruchio and Fredi Olster as Katherina

5: Scene: **I know...bright**: In Doran's 2003 RSC production, Katherina (Alexandra Gilbreath) started out confidently and aggressively, but her voice tailed away as she realized what would happen ("bright" was almost a whisper).

14: **rush candle**: weak candle made by dipping a rush in tallow or grease

Act 4, Scene 5]

PETRUCHIO
Come on a' God's name, once more toward our father's.
Good Lord, how bright and goodly shines the moon.

KATHERINA
The moon? The sun! It is not moonlight now.

PETRUCHIO
I say it is the moon that shines so bright.

KATHERINA
I know it is the sun that shines so bright.   5

PETRUCHIO
Now, by my mother's son, and that's myself,
It shall be moon or star or what I list,
Or e'er I journey to your father's house.
Go on, and fetch our horses back again,
Evermore crossed and crossed, nothing but crossed.   10

HORTENSIO
Say as he says, or we shall never go.

KATHERINA
Forward, I pray, since we have come so far,
And be it moon, or sun, or what you please;
And if you please to call it a rush candle,
Henceforth I vow it shall be so for me.   15

PETRUCHIO
I say it is the moon.

KATHERINA
                    I know it is the moon.

2-48:
Roger Allam as Petruchio and Frances Barber as Katherina
Marc Singer as Petruchio and Fredi Olster as Katherina

17: Scene: **Nay then...sun**: Penny Gay reports of Trevor Nunn's 1967 production with Michael Williams and Janet Suzman that Petruchio was clearly teasing Katherina and that she ended up laughing hysterically for a long time and lying prostrate on the ground when she said these words.

17: "Nay then you lie; it is the blessèd sun": Josie Lawrence as Katherina and Michael Siberry as Petruchio in the Royal Shakespeare Company's 1995 production directed by Gale Edwards
Photo: Donald Cooper

18: **is**: The First Folio reads "in"; the 1631 quarto first makes this emendation.

18–22: Scene: **Then...Katherine**: In Jonathan Miller's 1980 BBC film Katherina (Sarah Badel) said this with immense weariness and her head fell at the end.

25: **against the bias**: against its natural inclination (as in a game of lawn bowls)

35: Stage Direction: [*Aside*]: not in the First Folio; emendation first made by Capell (1768)

37: **where**: The First Folio reads "whether"; the Second Folio (1632) makes this emendation.

38–40: Scene: **so fair...bedfellow**: In Jonathan Miller's 1980 BBC film Petruchio (John Cleese) reached out to pluck Katherina's sleeve and continued to pull at it while she spoke. She finally turned to him as he spoke (line 41) and started to laugh so that she could hardly get out her next lines (44–48).

PETRUCHIO
Nay then you lie; it is the blessèd sun.

KATHERINA
Then God be blessed, it is the blessèd sun,
But sun it is not, when you say it is not,
And the moon changes even as your mind.   20
What you will have it named, even that it is,
And so it shall be so for Katherine.

HORTENSIO
Petruchio, go thy ways; the field is won.

PETRUCHIO
Well, forward, forward, thus the bowl should run,
And not unluckily against the bias.   25
But soft, company is coming here.

                                        Enter VINCENTIO

Good morrow, gentle mistress, where away?
Tell me sweet Kate, and tell me truly too,
Hast thou beheld a fresher gentlewoman?
Such war of white and red within her cheeks!   30
What stars do spangle heaven with such beauty
As those two eyes become that heavenly face?
Fair lovely maid, once more good day to thee.
Sweet Kate, embrace her for her beauty's sake.

HORTENSIO
[*Aside*] A will make the man mad, to make the woman of him.   35

KATHERINA
Young budding virgin, fair and fresh and sweet,
Whither away, or where is thy abode?
Happy the parents of so fair a child;
Happier the man whom favorable stars
Allots thee for his lovely bedfellow.   40

tracks 22-24

2-48:
Roger Allam as Petruchio and Frances Barber as Katherina
Marc Singer as Petruchio and Fredi Olster as Katherina

42: Scene: **old...withered**: In the 2007 Shakespeare Theatre Company Production directed by Taichman, Vincentio (Bill Hamlin) looked angry at these words and raised his stick threateningly at Petruchio (Christopher Innvar).

44-5: "Pardon, old father, my mistaking eyes / That have been so bedazzled with the sun": Elizabeth Taylor as Kate, Richard Burton as Petruchio, and Mark Dignam Vincentio in the 1967 film directed by Franco Zeffirelli © 1967 Columbia Pictures Corporation, Courtesy of Douglas Lanier

45: Scene: **That...sun**: In Doran's 2003 RSC production Katherina (Alexandra Gilbreath) hesitated at the last word and spoke it questioningly as she looked at Petruchio for confirmation that he was still calling it the sun.

46: **green**: fresh, young

63: **esteem**: reputation

65: **so qualified**: with such qualities; **beseem**: befit, be suitable for

PETRUCHIO
  Why, how now, Kate, I hope thou art not mad.
  This is a man, old, wrinkled, faded, withered,
  And not a maiden, as thou say'st he is.

KATHERINA
  Pardon, old father, my mistaking eyes
  That have been so bedazzled with the sun   45
  That everything I look on seemeth green.
  Now I perceive thou art a reverend father.
  Pardon, I pray thee, for my mad mistaking.

PETRUCHIO
  Do, good old grandsire, and withal make known
  Which way thou travelest. If along with us,   50
  We shall be joyful of thy company.

VINCENTIO
  Fair sir, and you, my merry mistress,
  That with your strange encounter much amazed me,
  My name is called Vincentio, my dwelling Pisa,
  And bound I am to Padua, there to visit   55
  A son of mine which long I have not seen.

PETRUCHIO
  What is his name?

VINCENTIO
                  Lucentio, gentle sir.

PETRUCHIO
  Happily met, the happier for thy son.
  And now by law, as well as reverend age,
  I may entitle thee my loving father.   60
  The sister to my wife, this gentlewoman,
  Thy son by this hath married. Wonder not,
  Nor be not grieved; she is of good esteem,
  Her dowry wealthy, and of worthy birth;
  Beside, so qualified, as may beseem   65

71: **break a jest**: play a practical joke

75: **jealous**: suspicious

75: Stage Direction: ***Exeunt. [Manet HORTENSIO.]***: The First Folio reads "*Exeunt*"; William Warburton (1747) first made this emendation.

77: **she be froward**: The First Folio reads "she froward"; the Second Folio (1632) makes this emendation.

78: **untoward**: stubborn, intractable, unruly

The spouse of any noble gentleman.
Let me embrace with old Vincentio,
And wander we to see thy honest son,
Who will of thy arrival be full joyous.

VINCENTIO
    But is this true, or is it else your pleasure,   70
    Like pleasant travelers to break a jest
    Upon the company you overtake?

HORTENSIO
    I do assure thee, father, so it is.

PETRUCHIO
    Come, go along and see the truth hereof,
    For our first merriment hath made thee jealous.   75
                    Exeunt. [Manet HORTENSIO.]

HORTENSIO
    Well, Petruchio, this has put me in heart.
    Have to my widow, and if she be froward,
    Then hast thou taught Hortensio to be untoward.
                                 Exit

[The Taming of the Shrew

the Shrew

Act 5

z.

o: no act or scene division here in First Folio; Warburton (1747) first made this division; Theobald (1733) also begins Act 5 here.

Set design from the Oregon Shakespeare Festival's 1991 production directed by Sandy McCallum
Set Design: Michael Ganio. Courtesy of the Oregon Shakespeare Festival

3: Stage Direction: *Exeunt [LUCENTIO and BIANCA]*: The First Folio reads "*Exit*"; Capell (1768) first made this emendation.

5: **master's**: The First Folio reads "mistris"; Capell (1768) first made this emendation.

8: **bears**: lies

Act 5, Scene 1]

Enter BIONDELLO, LUCENTIO and BIANCA.
GREMIO is out before

BIONDELLO
Softly and swiftly, sir, for the priest is ready.

LUCENTIO
I fly, Biondello. But they may chance to need thee at home; there-
fore leave us.
Exeunt [LUCENTIO and BIANCA]

BIONDELLO
Nay, faith, I'll see the church a' your back, and then come back
to my master's as soon as I can.   5
Exit BIONDELLO

GREMIO
I marvel Cambio comes not all this while.
Enter PETRUCHIO, KATHERINA, VINCENTIO,
GRUMIO, with Attendants

PETRUCHIO
Sir, here's the door. This is Lucentio's house;
My father's bears more toward the market-place.
Thither must I, and here I leave you, sir.

VINCENTIO
You shall not choose but drink before you go.   10
I think I shall command your welcome here,
And by all likelihood some cheer is toward.

Knock

GREMIO
They're busy within; you were best knock louder.
PEDANT looks out of the window

16: **withal**: with

22: **frivolous circumstances**: trivial details

29: **flat**: downright

PEDANT
What's he that knocks as he would beat down the gate?

VINCENTIO
Is Signor Lucentio within, sir?   15

PEDANT
He's within, sir, but not to be spoken withal.

VINCENTIO
What if a man bring him a hundred pound or two to make merry
withal?

PEDANT
Keep your hundred pounds to yourself; he shall need none so long
as I live.   20

PETRUCHIO
Nay, I told you your son was well beloved in Padua. Do you hear,
sir? To leave frivolous circumstances, I pray you tell Signor
Lucentio that his father is come from Pisa, and is here at the door
to speak with him.

PEDANT
Thou liest. His father is come from Padua and here looking out at   25
the window.

VINCENTIO
Art thou his father?

PEDANT
Ay, sir, so his mother says, if I may believe her.

PETRUCHIO
Why how now, gentleman! Why, this is flat knavery to take upon
you another man's name.   30

32: **under my countenance**: pretending to be me, using my good name

33: Stage Direction: [*Aside*]: not in the First Folio

34: **good shipping**: fair sailing or a good voyage, a conventional way of wishing good luck

35: **undone**: ruined

36: **crack-hemp**: gallows bird, rogue, one likely to die by being hanged

37: **I hope...choose**: I hope I may make my own decisions

41: **master's**: The First Folio reads "Mistris"; emendation first made in the Second Folio (1632).

PEDANT
    Lay hands on the villain. I believe a means to cozen some body in
    this city under my countenance.

Enter BIONDELLO

BIONDELLO
    [*Aside*] I have seen them in the church together, God send 'em
    good shipping! But who is here? Mine old Master Vincentio! Now
    we are undone and brought to nothing.   35

VINCENTIO
    Come hither, crack-hemp.

BIONDELLO
    I hope I may choose, sir.

VINCENTIO
    Come hither, you rogue. What, have you forgot me?

BIONDELLO
    Forgot you? No, sir. I could not forget you, for I never saw you
    before in all my life.   40

VINCENTIO
    What, you notorious villain, didst thou never see thy master's
    father, Vincentio?

BIONDELLO
    What, my old worshipful old master? Yes, marry, sir, see where he
    looks out of the window.

VINCENTIO
    Is't so indeed?   45

He beats BIONDELLO

BIONDELLO
    Help, help, help! Here's a mad man will murder me.

PEDANT
    Help, son! Help, signor Baptista!

48: "Prithee, Kate, let's stand aside and see the end of this controversy": Jay O. Sanders as Petruchio and Allison Janney as Kate in the 1999 Joseph Papp Public Theater production directed by Mel Shapiro
Photo: Michal Daniel

49: **offer**: presume

50: **fine**: richly dressed

52: **copatain hat**: high-crowned hat shaped like a sugar loaf

53: **good husband**: economical manager

57: **habit**: clothes

58: **'cerns**: concerns

59: **maintain**: afford

PETRUCHIO

Prithee, Kate, let's stand aside and see the end of this controversy.

Enter PEDANT with servants, BAPTISTA, [and] TRANIO

TRANIO

Sir, what are you that offer to beat my servant?

VINCENTIO

What am I, sir? Nay, what are you sir? Oh immortal gods! Oh fine   50
villain! A silken doublet, a velvet hose, a scarlet cloak, and a
copatain hat! Oh, I am undone, I am undone! While I play the
good husband at home, my son and my servant spend all at the
university.

TRANIO

How now, what's the matter?   55

BAPTISTA

What, is the man lunatic?

TRANIO

Sir, you seem a sober ancient gentleman by your habit, but your
words show you a madman. Why, sir, what 'cerns it you if I wear
pearl and gold? I thank my good father, I am able to maintain it.

VINCENTIO

Thy father! Oh villain, he is a sail-maker in Bergamo.   60

BAPTISTA

You mistake, sir, you mistake sir, pray what do you think is his
name?

VINCENTIO

His name? As if I knew not his name! I have brought him up ever
since he was three years old, and his name is Tranio.

PEDANT

Away, away, mad ass! His name is Lucentio and he is mine only   65
son and heir to the lands of me, Signor Vincentio.

64: **Tranio**: The First Folio reads "Tronio"; the Second Folio (1632) offers this emendation.

70: Stage Direction: *[Enter an Officer]*: not in the First Folio; Capell (1768) emended to *"Enter One with an Officer"*

72: **forthcoming**: ready to appear in court for trial

82: **dotard**: imbecile, stupid person

VINCENTIO
Lucentio! Oh, he hath murdered his master; lay hold on him, I
charge you in the Duke's name. Oh my son, my son! Tell me, thou
villain, where is my son Lucentio?

TRANIO
Call forth an officer.   70
[Enter an Officer]
Carry this mad knave to the jail. Father Baptista, I charge you see
that he be forthcoming.

VINCENTIO
Carry me to the jail?

GREMIO
Stay, officer. He shall not go to prison.

BAPTISTA
Talk not, Signor Gremio. I say he shall go to prison.   75

GREMIO
Take heed, Signor Baptista, lest you be cony-catched in this
business. I dare swear this is the right Vincentio.

PEDANT
Swear if thou dar'st.

GREMIO
Nay, I dare not swear it.

TRANIO
Then thou wert best say that I am not Lucentio.   80

GREMIO
Yes, I know thee to be Signor Lucentio.

BAPTISTA
Away with the dotard; to the jail with him.

Scott Denny as Lucentio and Erika Alexander as Bianca in the 1999 Joseph Papp Public Theater production directed by Mel Shapiro
Photo: Michal Daniel

83: **haled**: dragged around

83: Stage Direction: ***Enter BIONDELLO...BIANCA***: The direction follows "jail with him" (line 82) in the First Folio.

86: Stage Direction: ***[LUCENTIO and BIANCA] kneel***: The First Folio reads "*Kneele*"; Capell (1768) first made this emendation.

86–88: **Pardon...Here's Lucentio**: These lines are set as separate short lines in the First Folio (as opposed to shared lines as here).

91: **counterfeit...eyne**: false appearances tricked you

92: **packing...witness**: plotting, without a doubt

VINCENTIO
Thus strangers may be haled and abused. Oh monstrous villain!
Enter BIONDELLO, LUCENTIO and BIANCA

BIONDELLO
Oh, we are spoiled, and yonder he is. Deny him, forswear him, or
else we are all undone.   85
Exeunt BIONDELLO, TRANIO and PEDANT as fast as may be

LUCENTIO
Pardon, sweet Father.

[LUCENTIO and BIANCA] kneel

VINCENTIO
                         Lives my sweet son?

BIANCA
Pardon, dear Father.

BAPTISTA
                         How hast thou offended?
Where is Lucentio?

LUCENTIO
                         Here's Lucentio,
Right son to the right Vincentio,
That have by marriage made thy daughter mine,   90
While counterfeit supposes bleared thine eyne.

GREMIO
Here's packing, with a witness, to deceive us all.

VINCENTIO
Where is that damnèd villain, Tranio,
That faced and braved me in this matter so?

BAPTISTA
Why, tell me, is not this my Cambio?   95

107–108: Scene: **Fear...villainy**: In Jonathan Miller's 1980 BBC film Baptista (John Franklin-Robbins) was very angry and he and Vincentio (John Barron) departed enraged.

109: Scene: **And I...knavery**: In Doran's 2003 RSC production Bianca (Eve Myles) held out her hands to Baptista (Ian Gelder) but he pushed them away and exited, giving point to Lucentio's following line, "Look not pale, Bianca, thy father will not frown".

112: Stage Direction: *[Exit]*: not in the First Folio; emendation first made by Rowe (1709)

BIANCA
  Cambio is changed into Lucentio.

LUCENTIO
  Love wrought these miracles. Bianca's love
  Made me exchange my state with Tranio,
  While he did bear my countenance in the town,
  And happily I have arrived at the last   100
  Unto the wishèd haven of my bliss.
  What Tranio did, myself enforced him to;
  Then pardon him, sweet Father, for my sake.

VINCENTIO
  I'll slit the villain's nose that would have sent me to the jail.

BAPTISTA
  But do you hear, sir, have you married my daughter without   105
  asking my good will?

VINCENTIO
  Fear not, Baptista, we will content you. Go to. But I will in to be
  revenged for this villainy.

                                                                Exit

BAPTISTA
  And I to sound the depth of this knavery.

                                                                Exit

LUCENTIO
  Look not pale, Bianca, thy father will not frown.   110
                                                              Exeunt

GREMIO
  My cake is dough, but I'll in among the rest,
  Out of hope of all but my share of the feast.

                                                              [Exit]

KATHERINA
  Husband, let's follow, to see the end of this ado.

117: **No**: The First Folio reads "Mo"; the 1631 quarto makes this emendation.

119: Stage Direction: *[She kisses him]* : not in the First Folio; emendation first made by Capell (1768)

119: Scene: **Now pray thee, love, stay**: In Jonathan Miller's 1980 BBC film Katherina (Sarah Badel) grabbed Petruchio (John Cleese) for an enthusiastic kiss. In Bill Alexander's 1992 RSC production, Katherina (Amanda Harris) at first gave Petruchio (Anton Lesser) a quick, perfunctory kiss, but at this line, she reached out hesitantly for his hand, then gave him a long kiss whilst he put his arms around her. The lights went down while they were still wrapped in each other's arms and then came back up on the platform at the back. The play-watchers became increasingly restive as the (barely visible) kiss went on and on. After a while, more lights came back on to spotlight the couple as Petruchio said the next line, "Is not this well?" In Doran's 2003 RSC production, Katherina (Alexandra Gilbreath) and Petruchio (Jasper Britton) both made preparations, wiping their mouths and edging towards each other; the kiss continued until the audience finally started applauding. When he said, "Is not this well?" she laughed as she made the horizontal hand sign for "so-so," and it was clear that she was making a joke.

PETRUCHIO
First kiss me, Kate, and we will.

KATHERINA
What, in the midst of the street?   115

PETRUCHIO
What, art thou ashamed of me?

KATHERINA
No sir, God forbid, but ashamed to kiss.

PETRUCHIO
Why then, let's home again. Come, sirrah, let's away.

KATHERINA
Nay, I will give thee a kiss.

[She kisses him]

Now pray thee, love, stay.

PETRUCHIO
Is not this well? Come, my sweet Kate.   120
Better once than never, for never too late.

Exeunt

0: The First Folio reads *"Actus Quintus"*; George Steevens first made this scene division in 1773.

0: Stage Direction: ***Enter...banquet.***: The First Folio omits Petruchio, Katherina and Hortensio, lists Tranio twice and includes the Widow among the servants; Rowe (1709) first made this emendation.

2: **done**: The First Folio reads "come"; Rowe (1709) first made this emendation.

9: **close our stomachs up**: 1) finish off our meal and 2) perhaps also settle all our quarrels

10: **great good cheer**: i.e., the wedding feast

12: "Nothing but sit and sit, and eat and eat!": Jay O. Sanders as Petruchio in the 1999 Joseph Papp Public Theater production directed by Mel Shapiro
Photo: Michal Daniel

16: **fears**: frightens

17: **afeard**: afraid

Act 5, Scene 2]

Enter BAPTISTA, VINCENTIO, GREMIO, the PEDANT,
LUCENTIO, and BIANCA, [PETRUCHIO and KATHERINA],
[HORTENSIO] and WIDOW, TRANIO, BIONDELLO,
GRUMIO, with the Servingmen bringing in a banquet.

LUCENTIO
  At last, though long, our jarring notes agree,
  And time it is when raging war is done
  To smile at scapes and perils overblown.
  My fair Bianca, bid my father welcome,
  While I with selfsame kindness welcome thine.   5
  Brother Petruchio, sister Katherina,
  And thou, Hortensio, with thy loving widow,
  Feast with the best, and welcome to my house.
  My banquet is to close our stomachs up
  After our great good cheer. Pray you, sit down,   10
  For now we sit to chat as well as eat.

PETRUCHIO
  Nothing but sit and sit, and eat and eat!

BAPTISTA
  Padua affords this kindness, son Petruchio.

PETRUCHIO
  Padua affords nothing but what is kind.

HORTENSIO
  For both our sakes I would that word were true.   15

PETRUCHIO
  Now, for my life, Hortensio fears his widow.

WIDOW
  Then never trust me if I be afeard.

18: **sensible**: intelligent, endowed with good sense

21: **Roundly**: bluntly, outspokenly

22: **Thus I conceive by him**: this is the state I understand him to be in; Petruchio then takes the other sense of "conceive" concerning pregnancy.

31: **mean**: petty, small-minded

PETRUCHIO
  You are very sensible, and yet you miss my sense:
  I mean Hortensio is afeard of you.

WIDOW
  He that is giddy thinks the world turns round.   20

PETRUCHIO
  Roundly replied.

KATHERINA
                    Mistress, how mean you that?

WIDOW
  Thus I conceive by him.

PETRUCHIO
  Conceives by me! How likes Hortensio that?

HORTENSIO
  My widow says, thus she conceives her tale.

PETRUCHIO
  Very well mended. Kiss him for that, good widow.   25

KATHERINA
  He that is giddy thinks the world turns round,
  I pray you tell me what you meant by that.

WIDOW
  Your husband, being troubled with a shrew,
  Measures my husband's sorrow by his woe.
  And now you know my meaning.   30

KATHERINA
  A very mean meaning.

WIDOW
                    Right, I mean you.

Natasha Pyne as Bianca and Michael York as Lucentio in the 1967 film directed by Franco Zeffirelli
© 1967 Columbia Pictures Corporation, Courtesy of Douglas Lanier

32: respecting you: in comparison to you

35: put her down: Petruchio means that Katherina will defeat the widow, but Hortensio responds to the second possible meaning (i.e., to have sexual intercourse with her).

36: office: job, employment

37: thee: the First Folio reads "the"; the 1631 quarto makes this emendation.

39: butt together: butt their heads together

40: hasty witted body: precipitate or unduly quick person

41: head and horn: the horns on the head of the cuckold

45: bitter: The First Folio reads "better"; Capell (1768) first made this emendation.

KATHERINA
And I am mean indeed, respecting you.

PETRUCHIO
To her, Kate!

HORTENSIO
To her, widow!

PETRUCHIO
A hundred marks, my Kate does put her down.   35

HORTENSIO
That's my office.

PETRUCHIO
Spoke like an officer; ha' to thee, lad.

                                        Drinks to HORTENSIO

BAPTISTA
How likes Gremio these quick witted folks?

GREMIO
Believe me, sir, they butt together well.

BIANCA
Head, and butt! An hasty witted body   40
Would say your head and butt were head and horn.

VINCENTIO
Ay, mistress bride, hath that awakened you?

BIANCA
Ay, but not frighted me; therefore I'll sleep again.

PETRUCHIO
Nay, that you shall not. Since you have begun,
Have at you for a bitter jest or two.   45

46: **bird**: target; **shift my bush**: move to another bush

48: Stage Direction: ***Exeunt BIANCA, [KATHERINA and WIDOW]***: The First Folio reads *"Exit Bianca"*; Rowe (1709) first made this emendation.

52: **slipped me**: let me slip, unleashed me

54: **something currish**: somewhat like a cur (i.e., dog)

56: **does hold you at a bay**: turns on you like a hunted animal

58: **gird**: gibe, taunt

60: **galled**: vexed, chafed

62: **you two**: The First Folio reads "you too"; Rowe (1709) first made this emendation.

tracks 25-27

63-105: *Baptista, Petruchio, Hortensio, and Ensemble from the CBC Radio Adaptations series (1961)*
Norman Tyrrell as Baptista, Peter O'Toole as Petruchio, Richard Gale as Hortensio and Ensemble

63: **good sadness**: all seriousness

64: **veriest**: extremest, most complete

BIANCA
Am I your bird? I mean to shift my bush,
And then pursue me as you draw your bow.
You are welcome all.

Exeunt BIANCA, [KATHERINA and WIDOW]

PETRUCHIO
She hath prevented me. Here, Signor Tranio,
This bird you aimed at, though you hit her not.   50
Therefore a health to all that shot and missed.

TRANIO
Oh sir, Lucentio slipped me like his greyhound,
Which runs himself and catches for his master.

PETRUCHIO
A good swift simile, but something currish.

TRANIO
'Tis well, sir, that you hunted for yourself.   55
'Tis thought your deer does hold you at a bay.

BAPTISTA
Oh, oh, Petruchio, Tranio hits you now.

LUCENTIO
I thank thee for that gird, good Tranio.

HORTENSIO
Confess, confess, hath he not hit you here?

PETRUCHIO
'A has a little galled me, I confess,   60
And as the jest did glance away from me,
'Tis ten to one it maimed you two outright.

BAPTISTA
Now, in good sadness, son Petruchio,
I think thou hast the veriest shrew of all.

tracks 25-27

63-105: *Baptista, Petruchio, Hortensio, and Ensemble from the CBC Radio Adaptations series (1961)*
Norman Tyrrell as Baptista, Peter O'Toole as Petruchio, Richard Gale as Hortensio and Ensemble

65: for: The First Folio reads "sir"; the Second Folio (1632) makes this emendation; **assurance:** proof

71-73: "Twenty crowns? / I'll venture so much of my hawk or hound, / But twenty times so much upon my wife": Richard Burton as Petruchio and Elizabeth Taylor as Kate in the 1967 film directed by Franco Zeffirelli
© 1967 Columbia Pictures Corporation, Courtesy of Douglas Lanier

72: of: on

78: be your half: bear half your risk, take half your bet

PETRUCHIO
Well, I say no, and therefore for assurance,   65
Let's each one send unto his wife,
And he whose wife is most obedient
To come at first when he doth send for her,
Shall win the wager which we will propose.

HORTENSIO
Content. What's the wager?

LUCENTIO
                    Twenty crowns.   70

PETRUCHIO
Twenty crowns?
I'll venture so much of my hawk or hound,
But twenty times so much upon my wife.

LUCENTIO
A hundred then.

HORTENSIO
              Content.

PETRUCHIO
                    A match; 'tis done.

HORTENSIO
Who shall begin?

LUCENTIO
              That will I.   75
Go, Biondello, bid your mistress come to me.

BIONDELLO
I go.

                                                        Exit

BAPTISTA
Son, I'll be your half Bianca comes.

tracks 25-27

63-105: *Baptista, Petruchio, Hortensio, and Ensemble from the CBC Radio Adaptations series (1961)*
Norman Tyrrell as Baptista, Peter O'Toole as Petruchio, Richard Gale as Hortensio and Ensemble

Roger Rees as Petruchio in the 1999 Williamstown Theatre Festival
production directed by Roger Rees
Photo: Richard Feldman. Courtesy of Williamstown Theatre Festival

87: forthwith: immediately, without delay

LUCENTIO
I'll have no halves; I'll bear it all myself.

Enter BIONDELLO

How now, what news?

BIONDELLO
Sir, my mistress sends you word   80
That she is busy, and she cannot come.

PETRUCHIO
How? "She's busy, and she cannot come"?
Is that an answer?

GREMIO
Ay, and a kind one too.
Pray God, sir, your wife send you not a worse.

PETRUCHIO
I hope better.   85

HORTENSIO
Sirrah Biondello, go and entreat my wife
To come to me forthwith.

Exit BIONDELLO

PETRUCHIO
Oh ho, entreat her!
Nay then, she must needs come.

HORTENSIO
I am afraid, sir,
Do what you can, yours will not be entreated.

Enter BIONDELLO

Now, where's my wife?   90

BIONDELLO
She says you have some goodly jest in hand.
She will not come; she bids you come to her.

tracks 25-27

63-105: *Baptista, Petruchio, Hortensio, and Ensemble from the CBC Radio Adaptations series (1961)*
Norman Tyrrell as Baptista, Peter O'Toole as Petruchio, Richard Gale as Hortensio and Ensemble

97: Scene: **I know...She will not:** In production, Petruchio often looks quite uncertain during this exchange. In Franco Zeffirelli's 1967 film Richard Burton, despite all his bluster, looked unsure of what Katherina might say or do. In the 2007 Shakespeare Theatre Company Production, Petruchio (Christopher Innvar) had his face covered when Katherina (Charlayne Woodard) entered.

98: **fouler fortune mine:** worse luck for me

99: **holidame:** holiness

104: **Swinge:** beat, chastise

104–105: Scene: **Swinge me....straight:** In Bill Alexander's 1992 RSC production Katherina (Amanda Harris) went off rubbing her hands with pleased anticipation. In Doran's 2003 RSC production, Petruchio (Jasper Britton) tossed his sword to Katherina (Alexandra Gilbreath) who waved it about a bit before exiting with it.

105: Stage Direction: *[Exit KATHERINA]:* not in the First Folio; emendation first made by Rowe (1709)

PETRUCHIO
    Worse and worse: she will not come.
    Oh vile, intolerable, not to be endured.
    Sirrah Grumio, go to your mistress,   95
    Say I command her come to me.

                                                    Exit [GRUMIO]

HORTENSIO
    I know her answer.

PETRUCHIO
                        What?

HORTENSIO
                            She will not.

PETRUCHIO
    The fouler fortune mine, and there an end.

                                            Enter KATHERINA

BAPTISTA
    Now, by my holidame, here comes Katherina.

KATHERINA
    What is your will, sir, that you send for me?   100

PETRUCHIO
    Where is your sister, and Hortensio's wife?

KATHERINA
    They sit conferring by the parlor fire.

PETRUCHIO
    Go fetch them hither. If they deny to come,
    Swinge me them soundly forth unto their husbands;
    Away, I say, and bring them hither straight.   105
                                            [Exit KATHERINA]

LUCENTIO
    Here is a wonder, if you talk of a wonder.

109: **awful**: commanding respect or reverential fear

111: **fair befall thee**: good luck to you, congratulations

122: **bauble**: showy trinket or ornament

122: Stage Direction: ***[She obeys]*** : not in the First Folio; Rowe (1709) emends to "*She pulls off her Cap and throws it down*"

128: **a**: The First Folio reads "fiue"; Rowe (1709) made the first emendation to "an".

HORTENSIO
   And so it is; I wonder what it bodes.

PETRUCHIO
   Marry, peace it bodes, and love, and quiet life,
   An awful rule, and right supremacy,
   And to be short, what not, that's sweet and happy.   110

BAPTISTA
   Now fair befall thee, good Petruchio!
   The wager thou hast won, and I will add
   Unto their losses twenty thousand crowns,
   Another dowry to another daughter,
   For she is changed as she had never been.   115

PETRUCHIO
   Nay, I will win my wager better yet,
   And show more sign of her obedience,
   Her new built virtue and obedience.
                           Enter KATHERINA, BIANCA, and WIDOW
   See where she comes, and brings your froward wives
   As prisoners to her womanly persuasion.   120
   Katherine, that cap of yours becomes you not;
   Off with that bauble—throw it underfoot.
                                                           [She obeys]

WIDOW
   Lord, let me never have a cause to sigh
   Till I be brought to such a silly pass.

BIANCA
   Fie, what a foolish duty call you this?   125

LUCENTIO
   I would your duty were as foolish too.
   The wisdom of your duty, fair Bianca,
   Hath cost me a hundred crowns since supper time.

BIANCA
   The more fool you for laying on my duty.

130–131: Katherine...husbands: appears as prose in the First Folio; Rowe set these lines as verse in 1714.

132: you're: The First Folio reads "your"; the Third Folio (1663) makes this emendation.

tracks 28-31

136-180:
Sian Phillips as Katherina
Fredi Olster as Katherina
Frances Barber as Katherina

136–179: Scene: Fie, fie...ease: When Katherina begins her speech, Petruchio may be uncertain of her intent, despite her previous demonstrations of obedience. Sinead Cusack (Katherina in Barry Kyle's 1982 RSC production) has argued: "At the end of the play I was determined that Kate and Petruchio were rebels and would remain rebels for ever, so her speech was not predictable. Having invited her to speak, he couldn't know what form her rebellion was going to take. He was very shaky indeed in the scene, not knowing what was coming".

Much of the response to the play in performance will be strongly affected by the choices made about Katherina's speech. In Jonathan Miller's 1987 RSC production, when Grumio (Barrie Rutter) came back after being sent for Katherina (Fiona Shaw), he walked very slowly to and around the table. No Katherina was in sight and the men started to laugh until she entered. She sat down at the end of the table next to Petruchio (Brian Cox), took his hand, and delivered her speech very conversationally, partly speaking to Petruchio. When she got to "my hand is ready" she held it out to Petruchio who took and kissed it. Their subsequent kiss went on so long (through lines 181-183) that the others at the table got embarrassed and started shifting in their seats. In Gale Edwards' 1995 RSC production, when Katherina (Josie Lawrence), who was alone in the middle of the stage, got to "graceless traitor to her loving lord" (line 160), she reached out her arms towards Petruchio, but he stepped back. At line 169 ("Come, come, you froward and unable worms") she started to address her speech fiercely towards the audience, but her voice then got smaller as she turned to Petruchio briefly when she said lines 173-174 ("But now I see our lances are but straws..."). The speech ended with Katherina holding her hand out towards him as she sank lower, finally ending with her hand on the ground. He came towards her very slowly, dropping his winnings, and got down on one knee to put his hand near her, seeming crushed. She rose, and although he reached his hand towards her, she walked off, leaving him crouching. In Lindsay Posner's 1999 RSC production, Katherina (Monica Dolan) delivered her big speech straight, to the two women. At the end, she abased herself on the ground with her hand stretched out for Petruchio (Stuart McQuarrie) to step on. He sat frozen for a bit and then delivered his "Why there's a wench!" (line 180) as a triumphant roar to the other men.

140: Confounds thy fame: ruins your reputation
142: moved: angry
143: ill-seeming: of unpleasant appearance
150: watch: be on watch through

PETRUCHIO
    Katherine, I charge thee tell these head-strong women   130
    What duty they do owe their lords and husbands.

WIDOW
    Come, come, you're mocking: we will have no telling.

PETRUCHIO
    Come on, I say, and first begin with her.

WIDOW
    She shall not.

PETRUCHIO
    I say she shall, and first begin with her.   135

KATHERINA
    Fie, fie, unknit that threatening unkind brow,
    And dart not scornful glances from those eyes
    To wound thy lord, thy king, thy governor.
    It blots thy beauty, as frosts do bite the meads,
    Confounds thy fame, as whirlwinds shake fair buds,   140
    And in no sense is meet or amiable.
    A woman moved is like a fountain troubled,
    Muddy, ill-seeming, thick, bereft of beauty,
    And while it is so, none so dry or thirsty
    Will deign to sip, or touch one drop of it.   145
    Thy husband is thy lord, thy life, thy keeper,
    Thy head, thy sovereign, one that cares for thee,
    And for thy maintenance; commits his body
    To painful labor, both by sea and land,
    To watch the night in storms, the day in cold,   150
    Whil'st thou liest warm at home, secure and safe,
    And craves no other tribute at thy hands,
    But love, fair looks, and true obedience—
    Too little payment for so great a debt.
    Such duty as the subject owes the prince,   155
    Even such a woman oweth to her husband.

tracks 28-31

136-180:
Sian Phillips as Katherina
Fredi Olster as Katherina
Frances Barber as Katherina

160: **graceless**: depraved, ungodly
169: **unable worms**: powerless creatures
176: **vail...boot**: lower your pride for there is no help for it
179: **do him ease**: give him gratification

179: Scene: **My hand...ease**: Katherina's gesture, if any, and Petruchio's response are crucial to the interpretation of the play. In Jonathan Miller's 1980 BBC film, Petruchio (John Cleese) and Katherina (Sarah Badel) were sitting side by side at the table with the rest of the party; with these words Katherina placed her hand over his on the table. In Doran's 2003 RSC production, Petruchio (Jasper Britton) lifted his foot as he said "Come on" (line 180). Katherina (Alexandra Gilbreath) went over to put her hand under it, but he stopped her, and, kneeling, grabbed her to finish the line "and kiss me, Kate" with a sustained kiss and embrace. As they exited, Petruchio was putting his hand up her skirt, and she was shrieking.

180: Scene: **Come...Kate**: In Lindsay Posner's 1999 RSC production Petruchio (Stuart McQuarrie) stretched out his hand to raise Katherina (Monica Dolan) from the ground, and with his words, she leaped onto his lap and kissed him as Petruchio carried her offstage in his arms. The end of Gale Edwards' 1995 RSC production was quite different, as Michael Siberry (Petruchio) describes: "Kate, in our production, left Petruchio at the end of her speech. He understood and acknowledged that he had made a dreadful mistake and a permanent one—a mistake that cannot be undone. He fell to his knees, trying to make some sense of what had happened, understanding that he has made an awful mistake and trying to come to terms with it. But it is too late: Kate is receding, and the dream is fading. I dropped the bank-notes that had been wagered, and the cheque from Baptista, as I tried to move towards Kate, falling to my knees as she put out her hand on 'My hand is ready, may it do him ease' (line 179). But he couldn't take her hand after what she has just said; he just put his head in his own hands, aware of his terrible mistake and of the abuse of her trust, but not knowing what to do." (*Players*, 4).

181: **go thy ways**: go away, be on your way
182: **'Tis...toward**: it is good to hear when children are compliant
185: **sped**: ruined, done for

And when she is froward, peevish, sullen, sour,
And not obedient to his honest will,
What is she but a foul contending rebel,
And graceless traitor to her loving lord   160
I am ashamed that women are so simple,
To offer war where they should kneel for peace,
Or seek for rule, supremacy, and sway
When they are bound to serve, love, and obey.
Why are our bodies soft, and weak, and smooth   165
Unapt to toil and trouble in the world,
But that our soft conditions and our hearts
Should well agree with our external parts?
Come, come, you froward and unable worms,
My mind hath been as big as one of yours,   170
My heart as great, my reason haply more,
To bandy word for word, and frown for frown;
But now I see our lances are but straws,
Our strength as weak, our weakness past compare,
That seeming to be most, which we indeed least are.   175
Then vail your stomachs, for it is no boot,
And place your hands below your husband's foot.
In token of which duty, if he please,
My hand is ready; may it do him ease.

PETRUCHIO
    Why there's a wench! Come on, and kiss me, Kate.   180

LUCENTIO
    Well, go thy ways, old lad, for thou shalt ha't.

VINCENTIO
    'Tis a good hearing when children are toward.

LUCENTIO
    But a harsh hearing when women are froward.

PETRUCHIO
    Come, Kate, we'll to bed.
    We three are married, but you two are sped.   185

Bebe Neuwirth as Katherina and Roger Rees as Petruchio in the 1999
Williamstown Theatre Festival production directed by Roger Rees
Photo: Richard Feldman. Courtesy of Williamstown Theatre Festival

186: **hit the white**: hit the centre of the target (with an allusion to Bianca's name,
meaning white)

187: Stage Direction: ***Exeunt PETRUCHIO [and KATHERINA]***: The First Folio reads "*Exit*
PETRUCHIO"; Rowe (1709) made this emendation.

189: Scene: *FINIS*: As Alan Dessen has commented, using additional Sly material from
A Shrew "has provided an irresistible temptation for some directors" (*Rescripting
Shakespeare*, 185). In Bill Alexander's 1992 RSC production, after the main play finished,
the Lord got up from his position sitting at the fringes of the main-play picnic and
peered at the slumped Sly who was then carried out. The upper class characters from
the Induction walked onto and then off the stage. Sly was then brought back and
woken by the landlord. Sly then recounted his dream and told the landlord that he
now knew how to tame a shrew. In Lindsay Posner's 1999 RSC production, the last gesture of the play, following line 189 spoken by Lucentio (Jo Stone-Fewings), was Bianca
(Charlotte Randle) snatching his drink and downing it. The screen became visible again
at the back of the stage (the servants exited through the door in it) and a mechanical
voice said "connection terminated due to lack of network connectivity". Sly (Stuart
McQuarrie) was carried in and dumped unconscious on the stage; two women came
in (all in modern dress again now) and Sly gave the lines about his dream. He now
knew how to tame a shrew and went off to tame his wife (i.e., "tame her too").

'Twas I won the wager, though you hit the white,
And being a winner, God give you good night.

Exeunt PETRUCHIO [and KATHERINA]

HORTENSIO
Now go thy ways; thou hast tamed a curst shrew.

LUCENTIO
'Tis a wonder, by your leave, she will be tamed so.

FINIS.

A Voice Coach's Perspective on Speaking Shakespeare

KEEPING SHAKESPEARE PRACTICAL

Andrew Wade

tracks 35, 37

Introduction to Speaking Shakespeare: Sir Derek Jacobi
Speaking Shakespeare: Andrew Wade with Myra Lucretia Taylor

Why, you might be wondering, is it so important to keep Shakespeare practical? What do I mean by practical? Why is this the way to discover how to speak the text and understand it?

Plays themselves are not simply literary events—they demand interpreters in the deepest sense of the word, and the language of Shakespeare requires, therefore, not a vocal demonstration of writing techniques but an imaginative response to that writing. The key word here is imagination. The task of the voice coach is to offer relevant choices to the actor so that the actor's imagination is titillated, excited by the language, which he or she can then share with an audience, playing on that audience's imagination. Take the word "IF"—it is only composed of two letters when written, but if you say it aloud and listen to what it implies, then your reaction, the way the word plays through you, can change the perception of meaning. "Ifffffffff"… you might hear and feel it implying "possibilities," "choices," "questioning," "trying to work something out." The saying of this word provokes active investigation of thought. What an apt word to launch a play: "If music be the food of love, play on" (Act 1, Scene 1 in *Twelfth Night, or What You Will*). How this word engages the listener and immediately sets up an involvement is about more than audibility. How we verbalize sounds has a direct link to meaning and understanding. In the words of Touchstone in *As You Like It*, "Much virtue in if."

I was working with a company in Vancouver on *Macbeth,* and at the end of the first week's rehearsal—after having explored our voices and opening out different pieces of text to hear the possibilities of the rhythm, feeling how the meter affects the thinking and feeling, looking at structure and form— one of the actors admitted he was also a writer of soap operas and that I had completely changed his way of writing. Specifically, in saying a line like, "The multitudinous seas incarnadine / Making the green one red" he heard the complexity of meaning revealed in the use of polysyllabic words becoming monosyllabic, layered upon the words' individual dictionary definitions. The writer was reminded that merely reproducing the speech of everyday life was nowhere near as powerful and effective as language that is shaped.

Do you think soap operas would benefit from rhyming couplets? Somehow this is difficult to imagine! But, the writer's comments set me thinking. As I am constantly trying to find ways of exploring the acting process, of opening out actors' connection with language that isn't their own, I thought it would be a good idea to involve writers and actors in some practical work on language. After talking to Cicely Berry (Voice Director, the Royal Shakespeare Company) and Colin Chambers (the then RSC Production Adviser), we put together a group of writers and actors who were interested in taking part. It was a fascinating experience all round, and it broke down barriers and misconceptions.

The actors discovered, for instance, that a writer is not coming from a very different place as they are in their creative search; that an idea or an image may result from a struggle to define a gut feeling and not from some crafted, well-formed idea in the head. The physical connection of language to the body was reaffirmed. After working with a group on Yeats' poem *Easter 1916*, Ann Devlin changed the title of the play she was writing for the Royal Shakespeare Company to *After Easter*. She had experienced the poem read aloud by a circle of participants, each voice becoming a realization of the shape of the writing. Thus it made a much fuller impact on her and caused her thinking to shift. Such practical exchanges, through language work and voice, feed and stimulate my work to go beyond making sure the actors' voices are technically sound.

It is, of course, no different when we work on a Shakespeare play. A similar connection with the language is crucial. Playing Shakespeare, in many ways, is crafted instinct. The task is thus to find the best way to tap into someone's imagination. As Peter Brook put it, "People forget that a text is dumb. To make it speak, one must create a communication machine. A living network, like a nervous system, must be made if a text which comes from far away is to touch the sensibility of the present."

This journey is never to be taken for granted. It is the process that every text must undergo every time it is staged. There is no definitive rehearsal that would solve problems or indicate ways of staging a given play. Again, this is where creative, practical work on voice can help forge new meaning by offering areas of exploration and challenge. The central idea behind my work comes back to posing the question, "How does meaning change by speaking out aloud?" It would be unwise to jump hastily to the end process for, as Peter Brook says, "Shakespeare's words are records of the words that he wanted spoken, words issuing from people's mouths, with pitch, pause and rhythm and gesture as part of their meaning. A word does not start as a word—it is the end product which begins as an impulse, stimulated by attitude and behavior which dictates the need for expression" (1).

PRACTICALLY SPEAKING

Something happens when we vocalize, when we isolate sounds, when we start to speak words aloud, when we put them to the test of our physicality, of our anatomy. We expose ourselves in a way that makes taking the language back more difficult. Our body begins a debate with itself, becomes alive with the vibrations of sound produced in the mouth or rooted deep in the muscles that aim at defining sound. In fact, the spoken words bring into play all the senses, before sense and another level of meaning are reached.

"How do I know what I think, until I see what I say," Oscar Wilde once said. A concrete illustration of this phrase was reported to me when I was leading a workshop recently. A grandmother said the work we had done that day reminded her of what her six-year-old grandson had said to his mother while they were driving through Wales: "Look, mummy, sheep! Sheep! Sheep!" "You don't have to keep telling us," the mother replied, but the boy said, "How do I know they're there, if I don't tell you?!"

Therefore, when we speak of ideas, of sense, we slightly take for granted those physical processes which affect and change their meaning. We tend to separate something that is an organic whole. In doing so, we become blind to the fact that it is precisely this physical connection to the words that enables the actors to make the language theirs.

The struggle for meaning is not just impressionistic theater mystique; it is an indispensable aspect of the rehearsal process and carries on during the life of every production. In this struggle, practical work on Shakespeare is vital and may help spark creativity and shed some light on the way meaning is born into language. After a performance of *More Words*, a show devised and directed by Cicely Berry and myself, Katie Mitchell (a former artistic director of The Other Place in Stratford-upon-Avon) gave me an essay by Ted Hughes that echoes with the piece. In it, Ted Hughes compares the writing of a poem—the coming into existence of words—to the capture of a wild animal. You will notice that in the following passage Hughes talks of "spirit" or "living parts" but never of "thought" or "sense." With great care and precaution, he advises, "It is better to call [the poem] an assembly of living parts moved by a single spirit. The living parts are the words, the images, the rhythms. The spirit is the life which inhabits them when they all work together. It is impossible to say which comes first, parts or spirit."

This is also true of life in words, as many are connected directly to one or several of our senses. Here Hughes talks revealingly of "the five senses," of "word," "action," and "muscle," all things which a practical approach to language is more likely to allow one to perceive and do justice to.

Words that live are those which we hear, like "click" or "chuckle," or which we see, like "freckled" or "veined," or which we taste, like "vinegar" or "sugar," or touch, like "prickle" or "oily," or smell, like "tar" or "onion," words which belong to one of the five senses. Or words that act and seem to use their muscles, like "flick" or "balance" (2).

In this way, practically working on Shakespeare to arrive at understanding lends itself rather well, I think, to what Adrian Noble (former artistic director of the RSC) calls "a theater of poetry," a form of art that, rooted deeply in its classical origins, would seek to awaken the imagination of its audiences through love and respect for words while satisfying our eternal craving for myths and twice-told tales.

This can only be achieved at some cost. There is indeed a difficult battle to fight and hopefully to win: "the battle of the word to survive." This phrase was coined by Michael Redgrave at the beginning of the 1950s, a period when theater began to be deeply influenced by more physical forms, such as mime (3). Although the context is obviously different, the fight today is of the same nature.

LISTENING TO SHAKESPEARE

Because of the influence of television, our way of speaking as well as listening has changed. It is crucial to be aware of this. We can get fairly close to the way *Henry V* or *Hamlet* was staged in Shakespeare's time; we can try also to reconstruct the way English was spoken. But somehow, all these fall short of the real and most important goal: the Elizabethan ear. How did one "hear" a Shakespeare play? This is hardest to know. My personal view is that we will probably never know for sure. We are, even when we hear a Shakespeare play or a recording from the past, bound irrevocably to modernity. The Elizabethan ear was no doubt different from our own, as people were not spoken to or entertained in the same way. A modern voice has to engage us in a different way in order to make us truly listen in a society that seems to rely solely on the belief that image is truth, that it is more important to show than to tell.

Sometimes, we say that a speech in Shakespeare, or even an entire production, is not well-spoken, not up to standard. What do we mean by that? Evidently, there are a certain number of "guidelines" that any actor now has to know when working on a classical text. Yet, even when these are known, actors still have to make choices when they speak. A sound is not a sound without somebody to lend an ear to it: rhetoric is nothing without an audience.

There are a certain number of factors that affect the receiver's ear. These can be cultural factors such as the transition between different acting styles or the level of training that our contemporary ear has had. There are also personal and emotional factors. Often we feel the performance was not well-spoken because, somehow, it did not live up to our expectations of how we think it should have been performed. Is it that many of us have a self-conscious model, perhaps our own first experience of Shakespeare, that meant something to us and became our reference point for the future (some treasured performance kept under glass)? Nothing from then on can quite compare with that experience.

Most of the time, however, it is more complex than nostalgia. Take, for example, the thorny area of accent. I remind myself constantly that audibility is not embedded in Received Pronunciation or Standard American. The familiarity that those in power have with speech and the articulate confidence gained from coming from the right quarters can lead us all to hear certain types of voices as outshining others. But, to my mind, the role of theater is at least to question these assumptions so that we do not perpetuate those givens but work towards a broader tolerance.

In Canada on a production of *Twelfth Night*, I was working with an actor who was from Newfoundland. His own natural rhythms in speaking seemed completely at home with Shakespeare's. Is this because his root voice has direct links back to the voice of Shakespeare's time? It does seem that compared to British dialects, which are predominantly about pitch, many North American dialects have a wonderful respect and vibrancy in their use of vowels. Shakespeare's language seems to me very vowel-aware. How useful it is for an actor to isolate the vowels in the spoken words to hear the music they produce, the rich patterns, their direct connection to feelings. North Americans more easily respond to this and allow it to feed their speaking. I can only assume it is closer to how the Elizabethans spoke.

In *Othello* the very names of the characters have a direct connection to one vowel in particular. All the male names, except the Duke, end in the sound OH: Othello, Cassio, Iago, Brabantio, etc. Furthermore, the sound OH ripples through the play both consciously and unconsciously. "Oh" occurs repeatedly and, more interestingly, is contained within other words: "so," "soul," and "know." These words resonate throughout the play, reinforcing another level of meaning. The repetition of the same sounds affects us beyond what we can quite say.

Vowels come from deep within us, from our very core. We speak vowels before we speak consonants. They seem to reveal the feelings that require the consonants to give the shape to what we perceive as making sense.

Working with actors who are bilingual (or ones for whom English is not the native language) is fascinating because of the way it allows the actor to have an awareness of the cadence in Shakespeare. There seems to be an objective perception to the musical patterns in the text, and the use of alliteration and assonance are often more easily heard not just as literary devices, but also as means by which meaning is formed and revealed to an audience.

Every speech pattern (i.e., accent, rhythm) is capable of audibility. Each has its own music, each can become an accent when juxtaposed against another. The point at which a speech pattern becomes audible is in the dynamic of the physical making of those sounds. The speaker must have the desire to get through to a listener and must be confident that every speech pattern has a right to be heard.

SPEAKING SHAKESPEARE

So, the way to speak Shakespeare is not intrinsically tied to a particular sound; rather, it is how a speaker energetically connects to that language. Central to this is how we relate to the form of Shakespeare. Shakespeare employs verse, prose, and rhetorical devices to communicate meaning. For example, in *Romeo and Juliet*, the use of contrasts helps us to quantify Juliet's feelings: "And learn me how to lose a winning match," "Whiter than new snow upon a raven's back." These extreme opposites, "lose" and "winning," "new snow" and "raven's back," are her means to express and make sense of her feelings.

On a more personal note, I am often reminded how much, as an individual, I owe to Shakespeare's spoken word. The rather quiet and inarticulate schoolboy I once was found in the speaking and the acting of those words a means to quench his thirst for expression.

NOTES:

(1) Peter Brook, *The Empty Space* (Harmondsworth: Penguin, 1972)

(2) Ted Hughes, *Winter Pollen* (London: Faber and Faber, 1995)

(3) Michael Redgrave, *The Actor's Ways and Means*
   (London: Heinemann, 1951)

In the Age of Shakespeare

Thomas Garvey

One of the earliest published pictures of Shakespeare's birthplace, from an original watercolor by Phoebe Dighton (1834)

The works of William Shakespeare have won the love of millions since he first set pen to paper some four hundred years ago, but at first blush, his plays can seem difficult to understand, even willfully obscure. There are so many strange words: not fancy, exactly, but often only half-familiar. And the very fabric of the language seems to spring from a world of forgotten assumptions, a vast network of beliefs and superstitions that have long been dispelled from the modern mind.

In fact, when "Gulielmus filius Johannes Shakespeare" (Latin for "William, son of John Shakespeare") was baptized in Stratford-upon-Avon in 1564, English itself was only just settling into its current form; no dictionary had yet been written, and Shakespeare coined hundreds of words himself. Astronomy and medicine were entangled with astrology and the occult arts; democracy was waiting to be reborn; and even educated people believed in witches and fairies, and that the sun revolved around the Earth. Yet somehow Shakespeare still speaks to us today, in a voice as fresh and direct as the day his lines were first spoken, and to better understand both their artistic depth and enduring power, we must first understand something of his age.

Revolution and Religion

Shakespeare was born into a nation on the verge of global power, yet torn by religious strife. Henry VIII, the much-married father of Elizabeth I, had

From *The Book of Martyrs* (1563), this woodcut shows the Archbishop of Canterbury being burned at the stake in March 1556

Map of London ca. 1625

defied the Pope by proclaiming a new national church, with himself as its head. After Henry's death, however, his daughter Mary reinstituted Catholicism via a murderous nationwide campaign, going so far as to burn the Archbishop of Canterbury at the stake. But after a mere five years, the childless Mary also died, and when her half-sister Elizabeth was crowned, she declared the Church of England again triumphant.

In the wake of so many religious reversals, it is impossible to know which form of faith lay closest to the English heart, and at first, Elizabeth was content with mere outward deference to the Anglican Church. Once the Pope hinted her assassination would not be a mortal sin, however, the suppression of Catholicism grew more savage, and many Catholics—including some known in Stratford—were hunted down and executed, which meant being hanged, disemboweled, and carved into quarters. Many scholars suspect that Shakespeare himself was raised a Catholic (his father's testament of faith was found hidden in his childhood home). We can speculate about the impact this religious tumult may have had on his plays. Indeed, while explicit Catholic themes, such as the description of Purgatory in *Hamlet*, are rare, the larger themes of disguise and double allegiance are prominent across the canon. Prince Hal offers false friendship to Falstaff in the histories, the heroines of the comedies are forced to disguise themselves as men, and the action of the tragedies is driven by double-dealing villains. "I am not what I am," Iago tells us (and himself) in *Othello*, summing up in a single stroke what may have been Shakespeare's formative social and spiritual experience.

If religious conflict rippled beneath the body politic like some ominous undertow, on its surface the tide of English power was clearly on the rise. The defeat of the Spanish Armada in 1588 had established Britain as a global power; by 1595 Sir Walter Raleigh had founded the colony of Virginia (named for the Virgin Queen), and discovered a new crop, tobacco, which would inspire a burgeoning international trade. After decades of strife and the threat of invasion, England enjoyed a welcome stability. As the national coffers grew, so did London; over the course of Elizabeth's reign, the city would nearly double in size to a population of some 200,000.

Hornbook from Shakespeare's lifetime

A 1639 engraving of a scene from a royal state visit of Marie de Medici depicts London's packed, closely crowded half-timbered houses.

FROM COUNTRY TO COURT

The urban boom brought a new dimension to British life—the mentality of the metropolis. By contrast, in Stratford-on-Avon, the rhythms of the rural world still held sway. Educated in the local grammar school, Shakespeare was taught to read and write by a schoolmaster called an "abecedarian", and as he grew older, he was introduced to logic, rhetoric, and Latin. Like most schoolboys of his time, he was familiar with Roman mythology and may have learned a little Greek, perhaps by translating passages of the New Testament. Thus while he never attended a university, Shakespeare could confidently refer in his plays to myths and legends that today we associate with the highly educated.

Beyond the classroom, however, he was immersed in the life of the countryside, and his writing all but revels in its flora and fauna, from the wounded deer of *As You Like It* to the herbs and flowers which Ophelia

THE TAMING OF THE SHREW

scatters in *Hamlet*. Pagan rituals abounded in the rural villages of Shakespeare's day, where residents danced around maypoles in spring, performed "mummers' plays" in winter, and recited rhymes year-round to ward off witches and fairies.

The custom most pertinent to Shakespeare's art was the medieval "mystery play," in which moral allegories were enacted in country homes and village squares by troupes of traveling actors. These strolling players—usually four men and two boys who played the women's roles—often lightened the moralizing with bawdy interludes in a mix of high and low feeling, which would become a defining feature of Shakespeare's art. Occasionally even a professional troupe, such as Lord Strange's Men, or the Queen's Men, would arrive in town, perhaps coming straight to Shakespeare's door (his father was the town's bailiff) for permission to perform.

Rarely, however, did such troupes stray far from their base in London, the nation's rapidly expanding capital and cultural center. The city itself had existed since the time of the Romans (who built the original London Bridge), but it was not until the Renaissance that its population spilled beyond its ancient walls and began to grow along (and across) the Thames, by whose banks the Tudors had built their glorious palaces. It was these two contradictory worlds—a modern metropolis cheek-by-jowl with a medieval court—that provided the two very different audiences who applauded Shakespeare's plays.

Londoners both high and low craved distraction. Elizabeth's court constantly celebrated her reign with dazzling pageants and performances that required a local pool of professional actors and musicians. Beyond the graceful landscape of the royal parks, however, the general populace was packed into little more than a square mile of cramped and crooked streets where theatrical entertainment was frowned upon as compromising public morals.

Just outside the jurisdiction of the city fathers, however, across the twenty arches of London Bridge on the south bank of the Thames, lay the wilder district of "Southwark." A grim reminder of royal power lay at the end of the bridge—the decapitated heads of traitors stared down from pikes at passers-by. Once beyond their baleful gaze, people found the amusements they desired, and their growing numbers meant a market suddenly existed for daily entertainment. Bear-baiting and cockfighting flourished, along with taverns, brothels, and even the new institution of the theater.

Southwark, as depicted in Hollar's long view of London (1647). Blackfriars is on the top right and the labels of Bear-baiting and the Globe were inadvertently reversed.

THE ADVENT OF "THE THEATRE"

The first building in England designed for the performance of plays—called, straightforwardly enough, "The Theatre"—was built in London when Shakespeare was still a boy. It was owned by James Burbage, father of Richard Burbage, who would become Shakespeare's lead actor in the acting company the Lord Chamberlain's Men. "The Theatre," consciously or unconsciously, resembled the yards in which traveling players had long plied their trade—it was an open-air polygon, with three tiers of galleries surrounding a canopied stage in a flat central yard, which was ideal for the athletic competitions the building also hosted. The innovative arena must have found an appreciative audience, for it was soon joined by the Curtain, and then the Rose, which was the first theater to rise in Southwark among the brothels, bars, and bear-baiting pits.

Even as these new venues were being built, a revolution in the drama itself was taking place. Just as Renaissance artists turned to classical models for inspiration, so English writers looked to Roman verse as a prototype for the new national drama. "Blank verse," or iambic pentameter (that is, a poetic line with five alternating stressed and unstressed syllables), was an adaptation of Latin forms, and first appeared in England in a translation of Virgil's *Aeneid*. Blank verse was first spoken on stage in 1561, in the now-forgotten *Gorboduc*, but it was not until the brilliant Christopher Marlowe (born the same year as Shakespeare) transformed it into the "mighty line" of such plays as *Tamburlaine* (1587) that the power and flexibility of the form made it the baseline of English drama.

Marlowe—who, unlike Shakespeare, had attended college—led the "university wits," a clique of hard-living free thinkers who in between all manner of exploits managed to define a new form of theater. The dates of Shakespeare's arrival in London are unknown—we have no record of him in Stratford after 1585—but by the early 1590s he had already absorbed the essence of Marlowe's invention, and begun producing astonishing innovations of his own.

While the "university wits" had worked with myth and fantasy, however, Shakespeare turned to a grand new theme, English history—penning the three-part saga of *Henry VI* in or around 1590. The trilogy was such a success that Shakespeare became the envy of his circle—one unhappy competitor, Robert Greene, even complained in 1592 of "an upstart crow...beautified with our feathers...[who is] in his own conceit the only Shake-scene in a country."

Such jibes perhaps only confirmed Shakespeare's estimation of himself, for he began to apply his mastery of blank verse in all directions, succeeding at tragedy (*Titus Andronicus*), farce (*The Comedy of Errors*), and romantic comedy (*The Two Gentlemen of Verona*). He drew his plots from everywhere: existing poems, romances, folk tales, even other plays. In fact a number of Shakespeare's dramas (*Hamlet* included) may be revisions of earlier texts owned by his troupe. Since copyright laws did not exist, acting companies usually kept their texts close to their chests, only allowing publication when a play was no longer popular, or, conversely, when a play was *so* popular (as with *Romeo and Juliet*) that unauthorized versions had already been printed.

Demand for new plays and performance venues steadily increased. Soon, new theaters (the Hope and the Swan) joined the Rose in Southwark, followed shortly by the legendary Globe, which opened in 1600. (After some trouble with their lease, Shakespeare's acting troupe, the Lord

pendeſt on to meane a ſtay. Baſe minded men all thꝛee
of you,if by my miſerie you be not warnd:foꝛ vnto none
of you (like mee) ſought thoſe burres to cleaue : thoſe
Puppets (I meane)that ſpake from our mouths, thoſe
Anticks garniſht in our colours. Is it not ſtrange,that
I,to whom they all haue beene beholding: is it not like
that you,to whome they all haue beene beholding, ſhall
(were yee in that caſe as I am now) bee both at once of
them foꝛſaken ': Yes truſt them not : foꝛ there is an vp-
ſtart Crow, beautified with our feathers, that with his
Tygers hart wrapt in a Players hyde, ſuppoſes he is as
well able to bombaſt out a blanke verſe as the beſt of
you : and beeing an abſolute Iohannes fac totum, is in
his owne conceit the onely Shake-ſcene in a countrey.
O that I might intreat your rare wits to be imploied in
moꝛe pꝛofitable courſes : ꝓ let thoſe Apes imitate your
paſt excellence, and neuer moꝛe acquaint them with
your admired inuentions. I knowe the beſt huſband of

Greene's insult, lines 9–14

Chamberlain's Men, had disassembled "The Theatre" and transported its timbers across the Thames, using them as the structure for the Globe.) Shakespeare was a shareholder in this new venture, with its motto "All the world's a stage," and continued to write and perform for it as well. Full-length plays were now being presented every afternoon but Sunday, and the public appetite for new material seemed endless.

The only curb on the public's hunger for theater was its fear of the plague—for popular belief held the disease was easily spread in crowds. Even worse, the infection was completely beyond the powers of Elizabethan medicine, which held that health derived from four "humors" or internal fluids identified as bile, phlegm, blood, and choler. Such articles of faith, however, were utterly ineffective against a genuine health crisis, and in times of plague, the authorities' panicked response was to shut down any venue where large crowds might congregate. The theaters would be closed for lengthy periods in 1593, 1597, and 1603, during which times Shakespeare was forced to play at court, tour the provinces, or, as many scholars believe, write what would become his famous cycle of sonnets.

THE NEXT STAGE

Between these catastrophic closings, the theater thrived as the great medium of its day; it functioned as film, television, and radio combined as well as a venue for music and dance (all performances, even tragedies, ended with a dance). Moreover, the theater was the place to see and be seen; for a penny

Famous scale model of the Globe completed by Dr. John Cranford Adams in 1954. Collectively, 25,000 pieces were used in constructing the replica. Dr. Adams used walnut to imitate the timber of the Globe, plaster was placed with a spoon and medicine dropper, and 6,500 tiny "bricks" measured by pencil eraser strips were individually placed on the model.

you could stand through a performance in the yard, a penny more bought you a seat in the galleries, while yet another purchased you a cushion. The wealthy, the poor, the royal, and the common all gathered at the Globe, and Shakespeare designed his plays—with their action, humor, and highly refined poetry—not only to satisfy their divergent tastes but also to respond to their differing points of view. In the crucible of Elizabethan theater, the various classes could briefly see themselves as others saw them, and drama could genuinely show "the age and body of the time his form and pressure," to quote Hamlet himself.

In order to accommodate his expanding art, the simplicity of the Elizabethan stage had developed a startling flexibility. The canopied platform of the Globe had a trap in its floor for sudden disappearances, while an alcove at the rear, between the pillars supporting its roof, allowed for "discoveries" and interior space. Above, a balcony made possible the love scene in *Romeo and Juliet*; while still higher, the thatched roof could double as a tower or rampart. And though the stage was largely free of scenery, the costumes were sumptuous—a theater troupe's clothing was its greatest asset. Patrons were used to real drums banging in battle scenes and real cannons firing overhead (in fact, a misfire would one day set the Globe aflame).

With the death of Elizabeth, and the accession of James I to the throne in 1603, Shakespeare only saw his power and influence grow. James, who considered himself an intellectual and something of a scholar, took over the patronage of the Lord Chamberlain's Men, renaming them the King's Men; the troupe even marched in his celebratory entrance to London. At this pinnacle of both artistic power and prestige, Shakespeare composed *Othello*, *King Lear*, and *Macbeth* in quick succession, and soon the King's Men acquired a new, indoor theater in London, which allowed the integration of more music and spectacle into his work. At this wildly popular venue, Shakespeare developed a new form of drama that scholars have dubbed "the romance," which combined elements of comedy and tragedy in a magnificent vision that would culminate in the playwright's last masterpiece, *The Tempest*. Not long after this final innovation, Shakespeare retired to Stratford a wealthy and prominent gentleman.

BEYOND THE ELIZABETHAN UNIVERSE

This is how Shakespeare fit into his age. But how did he transcend it? The answer lies in the plays themselves. For even as we see in the surface of his drama the belief system of England in the sixteenth century, Shakespeare himself is always questioning his own culture, holding its ideas up to the light and shaking them, sometimes hard. In the case of the Elizabethan faith in astrology, Shakespeare had his villain Edmund sneer, "We make guilty of our disasters the sun, the moon, and stars; as if we were villains on necessity." When pondering the medieval code of chivalry, Falstaff decides, "The better part of valor is discretion." The divine right of kings is questioned in *Richard II*, and the inferior status of women—a belief that survived even the crowning of Elizabeth—appears ridiculous before the brilliant examples of Portia (*The Merchant of Venice*), and Rosalind (*As You Like It*). Perhaps it is through this constant shifting of perspective, this relentless sense of exploration, that the playwright somehow outlived the limits of his own period, and became, in the words of his rival Ben Jonson, "not just for an age, but for all time."

track 38

Conclusion of the Sourcebooks Shakespeare **The Taming of the Shrew**
Sir Derek Jacobi

About the Online Teaching Resources

The Sourcebooks Shakespeare is committed to supporting students and educators in the study of Shakespeare. A website with additional articles and essays, extended audio, a forum for discussions, as well as other resources can be found (starting in August 2006) at www.sourcebooksshakespeare.com. To illustrate how the Sourcebooks Shakespeare may be used in your class, Jeremy Ehrlich, the head of education at the Folger Shakespeare Library, contributed an essay called "Working with Audio in the Classroom." The following is an excerpt:

One possible way of approaching basic audio work in the classroom is shown in the handout [on the site]. It is meant to give some guidance for the first-time user of audio in the classroom. I would urge you to adapt this to the particular circumstances and interests of your own students.

To use it, divide the students into four groups. Assign each group one of the four technical elements of audio—volume, pitch, pace, and pause—to follow as you play them an audio clip or clips. In the first section, have them record what they hear: the range they encounter in the clip and the places where their element changes. In the second section, have them suggest words for the tone of the passage based in part on their answers to the first. Sections three and four deal with tools of the actor. Modern acting theory finds the actor's objective is his single most important acting choice; an actor may then choose from a variety of tactics in order to achieve that objective. Thus, if a character's objective on stage is to get sympathy from his scene partner, he may start out by complaining, then shift to another tactic (asking for sympathy directly? throwing a tantrum?) if the first tactic fails. Asking your students to try to explain what they think a character is trying to get, and how she is trying to do it, is a way for them to follow this process through closely. Finally, the handout asks students to think about the meaning (theme) of the passage, concluding with a traditional and important tool of text analysis.

As you can see, this activity is more interesting and, probably, easier for students when it's used with multiple versions of the same piece of text. While defining an actor's motivation is difficult in a vacuum, doing so in relation to another performance may be easier: one Othello may be more concerned with gaining respect, while another Othello may be more concerned with obtaining love, for instance. This activity may be done outside of a group setting, although for students doing this work for the first time I suggest group work so they will be able to share answers on some potentially thought-provoking questions...

For the complete essay, please visit www.sourcebooksshakespeare.com.

Acknowledgments

The series editors wish to give heartfelt thanks to the advisory editors of the series, David Bevington and Peter Holland, for their ongoing support, timely advice, and keen brilliance.

We are incredibly grateful to the community of Shakespeare scholars for their generosity in sharing their talents, collections, and even their address books. We would not have been able to put together such an august list of contributors without their help. First, sincere thanks to our text editor, Antonia Forster, for her thorough work. Thanks as well to Christy Desmet, Tom Garvey, Doug Lanier, and Andrew Wade for their marvelous essays. Extra appreciation goes to Doug Lanier for the use of his personal Shakespeare collection. We are grateful to William Williams for his continuing guidance on textual issues, though any errors in this edition are ours.

Our research was aided immensely by the wonderful staff at Shakespeare archives and libraries around the world: Susan Brock, Helen Hargest, and the staff at The Shakespeare Birthplace Trust; Jeremy Ehrlich, Bettina Smith, and everyone at the Folger Shakespeare Library; Jessica Talmage at the Mary Evans Picture Library; and Gene Rinkel, Bruce Swann, and Tim Cole from the Rare Books and Special Collections Library at the University of Illinois. These individuals were instrumental in helping us gather audio: Justyn Baker, Janet Benson, Barbara Brown, Lylian Morcos, and Traci Cothran. The following are the talented photographers who shared their work with us: Donald Cooper, George Joseph, Michal Daniel, Carol Pratt, and Carol Rosegg. The set and costume designers from the Oregon Shakespeare Festival (Susan E. Mickey, Michael Ganio, Kent Dorsey) generously gave us permision to use their wonderful designs. We appreciate all their help.

From the world of drama, the following shared their passion with us and helped us develop the series into a true partnership between the artistic and academic communities. We are indebted to: Liza Lorenz, Lauren Beyea, and the team from the Shakespeare Theatre Company; Amy Richard and the team at the Oregon Shakespeare Festival; Nancy Becker of The Shakespeare Society; and Myra Lucretia Taylor.

With respect to the audio, we extend our heartfelt thanks to our narrating team: our director, John Tydeman, our esteemed narrator, Sir Derek Jacobi, and the staff of Motivation Studios. John has been a wonderful, generous resource to us and we look forward to future collaborations. We owe a debt of gratitude to Nicolas Soames for introducing us and for being unfailingly helpful. Thanks also to the "Speaking Shakespeare" team: Andrew Wade and Myra Lucretia Taylor for that wonderful recording. Thanks to Joe Plummer for his keen audio analysis, without whom we could not write the script. We are also very grateful to Fredi Olster and Marc Singer for their support of the series and for granting us permission to use their wonderful performances.

Our personal thanks for their kindness and unstinting support go to our friends and our extended families. We also want to thank Tanya Gough, the founder of The Poor Yorick Shakespeare Catalog, for all her efforts on behalf of the series.

Finally, thanks to everyone at Sourcebooks who contributed their talents in realizing The Sourcebooks Shakespeare. Special mention to Tiffany Breyne, Eileen Foley, and Elizabeth Lhost, assistants extraordinaire for the Sourcebooks Shakespeare.

So, thanks to all at once and to each one (Macbeth, 5.7.104)

Audio Credits

In all cases, we have attempted to provide archival audio in its original form. While we have tried to achieve the best possible quality on the archival audio, some audio quality is the result of source limitations. Archival audio research by Marie Macaisa. Narration script by Joe Plummer and Marie Macaisa. Audio editing by Motivation Sound Studios, Marie Macaisa, and Todd Stocke. Narration recording and audio engineering by Motivation Sound Studios, London, UK. Mastering by Paul Estby. Recording for "Speaking Shakespeare" by Dubway Studios, New York City, USA.

Narrated by Sir Derek Jacobi
Directed by John Tydeman
Produced by Marie Macaisa

The following are courtesy of Thirteen/WNET New York. All rights reserved. Tracks 12, 24, 30

The following are under license from CBC Radio. All rights reserved. Tracks 18, 20, 26

The following are under license from IPC Media. All rights reserved. Tracks 3, 6, 8, 15, 27, 29

The following are selections from The Complete Arkangel Shakespeare (p) 2003, with permission of BBC Audiobooks America. All rights reserved. Copyright exists on all recordings issued by BBC Audiobooks America. Any unauthorized broadcasting, public performance, copying or re-recording of such recordings in any manner whatsoever, will constitute an infringement of such copyright.

Tracks 4, 9, 11, 14, 17, 21, 23, 31

Photo Credits

Photos from the Shakespeare Theatre Company's 1994-1995 production directed by Adrian Hall are © 1994-95 Carol Pratt.

Photos from the Williamstown Theatre Festival's 1999 production directed by Roger Rees are © 1999 Richard Feldman and courtesy of Roger Rees and the Williamstown Theatre Festival.

Photos from the Oregon Shakespeare Festival's 1991 production directed by Sandy McCallum are courtesy of the Oregon Shakespeare Festival; set design by Michael Ganio. Costume renderings from the 2000 production directed by Kenneth Albers are courtesy of the Oregon Shakespeare Festival; costume design by Susan E. Mickey; set design by Kent Dorsey.

William Shakespeare's signature (on the title page) courtesy of Mary Evans Picture Library. Other images from the Mary Evans Picture Library used in the text are credited on the pages in which they appear.

Images from "In the Age of Shakespeare" courtesy of The Folger Shakespeare Library.

About the Contributors

TEXT EDITOR

Antonia Forster is Professor of English at the University of Akron. Her *Index to Book Reviews in England 1749-1774* was awarded the 1992 Rose Mary Crawshay Prize by the British Academy, and the second volume to take the Index to 1800 was published by the British Library in 1997. Her Vol. 1 (1770-1799) of *The English Novel 1770-1829: a Bibliographical Survey of Prose Fiction Published in the British Isles* (with James Raven) was published by Oxford University Press in 2000. She has published articles in such journals as *The Age of Johnson, Shakespeare Quarterly*, and *Studies in Newspaper and Periodical History*, and has been awarded fellowships for research in the Folger, Newberry, Houghton, Beinecke and British Libraries. She is also preparing an edition of the correspondence of Ralph Griffiths, founding editor of the *Monthly Review*.

SERIES EDITORS

Marie Macaisa has a bachelor's degree in computer science from the Massachusetts Institute of Technology and a master's degree in artificial intelligence from the University of Pennsylvania. She worked for many years on the research and development of innovative applications of computer technology before becoming the series editor of *The Sourcebooks Shakespeare* in 2003. She contributed the *Cast Speaks* essays for previous volumes and is the producer of the accompanying audio CDs.

Dominique Raccah is the founder, president, and publisher of Sourcebooks. Born in Paris, France, she has a bachelor's degree in psychology and a master's in quantitative psychology from the University of Illinois. She also serves as series editor of *Poetry Speaks* and *Poetry Speaks to Children*.

ADVISORY BOARD

David Bevington is the Phyllis Fay Horton Distinguished Service Professor in the Humanities at the University of Chicago. A renowned text scholar, he has edited several Shakespeare editions including the *Bantam Shakespeare* in individual paperback volumes, *The Complete Works of Shakespeare* (Long-man, 2003), and *Troilus and Cressida* (Arden, 1998). He teaches courses in Shakespeare, renaissance drama, and medieval drama.

Peter Holland is the McMeel Family Chair in Shakespeare Studies at the University of Notre Dame. One of the central figures in performance-oriented Shakespeare criticism, he has also edited many Shakespeare plays, including *A Midsummer Night's Dream* for the Oxford Shakespeare series. He is also general editor of Shakespeare Survey and co-general editor (with Stanley Wells) of Oxford Shakespeare Topics. Currently he is completing a book, *Shakespeare on Film*, and editing *Coriolanus* for the Arden 3rd series.

ESSAYISTS

Christy Desmet is Associate Professor of English at the University of Georgia. Her numerous publications include her book, *Reading Shakespeare's Characters: Rhetoric, Ethics, and Identity* (University of Massachusetts Press, 1992) and journal articles in *Upstart Crow 26 (2006-2007), Shakespeare Studies 34* (2006) and *Journal of Educational Computing Research* (2004). She is the co-editor of *Harold Bloom's Shakespeare* (Ed. Christy Desmet and Robert Sawyer, New York: Palgrave, 2001), and is the co-founder and co-general editor of *Borrowers and Lenders: The Journal of Shakespeare and Appropriation*.

Douglas Lanier is an associate professor of English at the University of New Hampshire. He has written many essays on Shakespeare in popular culture, including "Shakescorp Noir" in *Shakespeare Quarterly 53.2* (Summer 2002) and "Shakespeare on the Record" in *The Blackwell Companion to Shakespeare in Performance* (edited by Barbara Hodgdon and William Worthen, Blackwell, 2005). His book *Shakespeare and Modern Popular Culture* (Oxford University Press) was published in 2002. He is currently working on a book-length study of cultural stratification in early modern British theater.

Thomas Garvey has been acting, directing, or writing about Shakespeare for over two decades. A graduate of the Massachusetts Institute of Technology, he studied acting and directing with the MIT Shakespeare Ensemble, where he played Hamlet, Jacques, Iago, and other roles, and directed *All's Well That*

Ends Well and *Twelfth Night*. He has since directed and designed several other Shakespearean productions, as well as works by Chekhov, Ibsen, Sophocles, Beckett, Moliere, and Shaw. Mr. Garvey has written on theatre for the *Boston Globe* and other publications.

Andrew Wade was head of voice for the Royal Shakespeare Company from 1990 to 2003 and voice assistant director from 1987 to 1990. During this time he worked on 170 productions and with more than 80 directors. Along with Cicely Berry, Andrew recorded *Working Shakespeare* and the DVD series on *Voice and Shakespeare*, and he was the verse consultant for the movie *Shakespeare In Love*. In 2000, he won a Bronze Award from the New York International Radio Festival for the series *Lifespan*, which he co-directed and devised. He works widely teaching, lecturing, and coaching throughout the world.

AUDIO CONTRIBUTORS

Sir Derek Jacobi (Series Narrator) is one of Britain's foremost actors of stage and screen. One of his earliest Shakespearean roles was Cassio to Sir Laurence Olivier's Othello in Stuart Burge's 1965 movie production. More recent roles include Hamlet in the acclaimed BBC Television Shakespeare production in 1980, the Chorus in Kenneth Branagh's 1989 film of *Henry V*, and Claudius in Branagh's 1996 movie *Hamlet*. He has been accorded numerous honors in his distinguished career, including a Tony award for Best Actor in *Much Ado About Nothing* and a BAFTA (British Academy of Film and Television) for his landmark portrayal of Emperor Claudius in the blockbuster television series *I, Claudius*. He was made a Knight of the British Empire in 1994 for his services to the theatre.

Joe Plummer (Audio Analyst) is the Director of Education for the Williamstown Theatre Festival and Assistant Professor of Shakespearean Performance with Roger Rees at Fordham University's Lincoln Center campus. He has taught several Master classes on Shakespeare and performance at Williams College, the National Shakespeare Company and Brandeis University, and also teaches privately. Joe is currently the Artist-In-Residence and Director of Educational Outreach for The Shakespeare Society in New York City and is the founder and Producing Artistic Director of poortom productions, the only all-male Shakespeare Company in the U.S. He has performed extensively in New York and in regional theaters.

John Tydeman (Series Director) was the Head of Drama for BBC Radio for many years and is the director of countless productions, with 15 Shakespeare plays to his credit. Among his numerous awards are the Prix Italia, Prix Europa, UK Broadcasting Guild Best Radio Programme (*When The Wind Blows* by Raymond Briggs), and the Sony Personal Award for services to radio. He has worked with most of Britain's leading actors and dramatists and has directed for the theatre, television, and commercial recordings. He holds an M.A. from Cambridge University.